Spanish with Carlos

Charlie de Wirtz

A self-study beginners guide to Spanish

FIRST EDITION

Acknowledgements

The author would like to acknowledge the assistance and patience of the following people:

An Young-Hee
Jane Prior
Michael Duxbury
Maureen Baker
Ruth de Wirtz

First published in 2003
by Luxan Publishers
7 Upper Carlisle Road Eastbourne
East Sussex BN20 7TN

© Luxan Publishers

Website: www.spanishwithcarlos.com / co.uk

ISBN: 0 9546088-0-1

A catalogue record for this book is available from the British Library.

Contents

Introduction

Welcome to **Spanish with Carlos**. What you are holding in your hands is an extremely clear and user-friendly introduction into Spanish. For any newcomers to the language, or anyone wishing really to establish their grasp of the basics, this course is the ideal place to start.

It doesn't claim magical formulas for language learning, nor make unrealistic promises like "You'll be able to speak fluently within three months." Instead, the purpose here is to provide you with an essential overview of how Spanish works as a language, and to explain the basics in a systematic and easy-to-understand fashion. **Spanish with Carlos** will give you a firm foundation on which to build, a foundation which you will come to see is essential if you really want to get to grips with the language.

One of the things that people need to realize when they study a language for the first time is just how difficult it really is. If you have ever studied another language, you will know this already. It is better to be under no illusions from the start. It is a long process that requires hard work and commitment. There are no shortcuts.

Of course, if you have got as far as reading this, you are considering giving it a go. Whether you are starting for the first time, or whether you have tried several times before and given up (there are many students of whom that is true!) the way in which the material in this course is presented inspires confidence through its easy-to-read style. Confidence is the key to many things in life, and learning a language is no exception.

Some people have a mental block about learning a language, and get the idea fixed in their minds that try as they might, they won't be able to crack it. Studying this course will not mean that you can suddenly 'magically' speak Spanish – no course can achieve that – but I hope it will mean that any doubts you may have regarding your own ability to learn Spanish will be removed. **Spanish with Carlos** will give you not only the basis, but also the belief, on which to build.

The material is presented in a clear, easy-to-study fashion. Both audio and written material are used. Studying alone has its disadvantages, but it has advantages too. Some people become very self-conscious when they study in a group, and can get quite nervous about the thought of participating – especially when it comes to actually having to speak in Spanish. Here, you will be able to practise the pronunciation exercises alone, within the comfort and relaxed atmosphere of your own home. Having said that, the point of practice is to get you ready to communicate in real life situations, so at some point you will have to leave the comfort of your own company and get out there!

Frequently throughout the course book you will be instructed to use the accompanying CDs. They serve to reiterate certain key points, teach pronunciation techniques and provide plenty of listening practice. Both the written and audio material is clear and easy to follow. To make it easy to find and re-find relevant parts of the audio material, the CDs are broken down into tracks which are numbered. They are clearly indicated in the written material.

Don't be put off by the Module titles or the Key Grammar Terms that appear in boxes at the beginning of most Modules. You will almost certainly come across some terms and phrases that you are unfamiliar with. As you read on however, everything will be explained. The Key Grammar terms are there for you to refer back to, as and when you need.

Please don't be offended at my definitions of terms like adjectives and verbs. Teachers quickly learn that it is best to assume ignorance. If you are one of those for whom the difference between an adjective and a verb is clear, then be grateful for your knowledge, skip my explanations, and get on with the rest of the course!

I always liken learning a language to building a house. If you want the final result to be good, you have to do things in the right order. You have to start by laying a good, solid foundation which will give you a reference point for all subsequent learning. **Spanish with Carlos** will give you that invaluable base, and set you firmly on the path to learning Spanish.

Go into the course armed with the mindset that there is nothing here that is beyond you to understand and absorb. With perseverance, I am sure you will be able to comprehend all the concepts taught here and put them into practice.

Enjoy it – and good luck!

About the Author

Charlie de Wirtz is an experienced language teacher who has a diploma in Spanish acquired through studying with the Open University. Having a father who was half-Spanish served to fuel his interest in Spanish life, language and culture. Although he grew up and was educated in England, he has lived in several other countries (including a three-year spell on the Costa del Sol in Spain) and has travelled extensively.

He has written a large amount of language material for teachers and students and in the late 1990s built and ran his own language school for foreign students learning English and English people learning Spanish. Among family members and his many Spanish friends he is affectionately known as "Carlos" – hence the title of the course.

Further Points

■ The Key Grammar Terms required are listed in a box at the beginning of each Module, and are written in bold every time they appear in the rest of that Module.

■ After every four Modules there is a Progress Check (four in all) which provides further practice exercises combining everything studied up until that point.

■ You will need a dictionary to do this course. In many of the examples I have used words that have already come up in the course, but to increase your vocabulary and get you doing things for yourself, I have also used some new words at times which, if you don't know, you will need to look up.

■ There are Practice Activities throughout the course – I strongly suggest that you don't write the answers in the book but use a separate sheet of paper – that way you can do and re-do the exercises as many times as you want to in the future.

■ There is an Answers Section at the back in which you can find all the answers to the questions in the Practice Activities and the Progress Checks.

■ I strongly recommend that you don't study more than one Module at a time. Although some of them may not take long to read, they nevertheless contain a lot of information. It's better to try and assimilate that information before moving on.

THE PRESENT SIMPLE

KEY GRAMMAR TERMS

PRESENT SIMPLE	The tense that translates as *I do* something.
VERB	A word which describes an action, a doing word.
REGULAR VERB	A verb which follows the normal pattern in how its different parts are formed.
INFINITIVE	The part of the verb that is preceded by *to*.
GERUND	The part of the verb that adds "ing" on the end.
STEM	The part of the verb minus its ending (also called the *root*).
ENDING	Whatever is placed on the end of the stem to form a different part of the verb.
SUBJECT PRONOUNS	The words that mean *I, you, he, she, it, we, you, they*.

A **verb** means a doing word, a word that describes some action.
Sleep, *buy* and *go* are all examples of **verbs**, because they describe an action.
Let's start by learning the names of two parts of a **verb**.

To do something is called the **infinitive**, and *doing* something is called the **gerund**.

So, *to sleep*, *to buy* and *to go* are all examples of **infinitives**, whereas *sleeping*, *buying* and *going* are all examples of **gerunds**.

In this Module, all you need to remember is what the **infinitive** means.

Whenever the word is used throughout this course, remember that it refers to the part of the **verb** that sticks *to* in front of it.

In Spanish there are three kinds of **verbs** - one that ends in the letters AR, one that ends in the letters ER and one that ends in the letters IR
All **verbs** in Spanish fall into one of these three categories.

Here's an example of each kind, written in the **infinitive** form, with the English translation in brackets:

> MIRAR (*to look at*)   COMER (*to eat*)   VIVIR (*to live*)

These **verbs** are in the **infinitive** form. Every **infinitive** in Spanish ends in either AR or ER or IR.
And these three examples are all **regular verbs**.

Don't worry at this stage if the term **regular verb** doesn't make sense to you. By the end of this Module it will.

The purpose of this first Module is to teach you how to form the **Present Simple** tense.

So far you have learnt that the **infinitive** means *to do* something.
Mirar, therefore, means *to look at*.

The **Present Simple** means learning how to say *somebody does* something.

Have a look at the following examples of the **Present Simple** in English:

I smoke	They talk
He writes	She goes
We eat	You buy

These are all examples of the **Present Simple** tense.

To form the **Present Simple** of **regular verbs** in Spanish, we have to split the **infinitive** into two parts. Look at the split that is indicated next in our AR **verb**:

> MIR–AR

The MIR part I am going to call the **stem** or root. The AR part we can call the **ending**.

In Spanish, when we want to express a **regular verb** in the **Present Simple**, we do it by removing the **ending** (either "ar", "er" or "ir") from the **stem**, and adding different **endings**, each of which denotes a different person who does the action.

Let's take the case of our model (**regular**) AR **verb** first, Mirar

MODEL – AR VERB

MIR-O	means	I look at
MIR-AS	means	You look at
MIR-A	means	He / She / It looks at
MIR-AMOS	means	We look at
MIR-ÁIS	means	You look at
MIR-AN	means	They look at

Notice how that for each person a different **ending** has been added.

Don't make the mistake of thinking that the **ending** "o" means *I*, and the **ending** "as" means *you*, etc, because they don't.

It is simply that those **endings** denote who is doing the action of the **verb**.

The words in Spanish which mean *I, you, he, she, it, we, you* and *they* are called **subject pronouns**, and you will learn them in a moment.

Notice in the **verb** Mirar how the **stem** stays the same throughout, but the **endings** are always different. I have inserted a hyphen in order to highlight this. It is from the **ending** of the **verb** that we can tell who is doing the action of the **verb**.

There are, therefore, two characteristics of a **regular verb** in Spanish:

■ The **stem** (which you get after removing the **ending** of the **infinitive**) remains the same throughout the **Present Simple** tense.

■ A set of **endings** are attached to the **stem**, each one of which is different and each one of which denotes who is doing the action of the **verb**.

Exactly the same principle applies for **regular** ER and IR **verbs**, although the **endings** that are added are different for each category.

You can see this from the examples of Comer and Vivir which follow now.

MODEL – ER VERB

COM-O	means	I eat
COM-ES	means	You eat
COM-E	means	He / She / It eats
COM-EMOS	means	We eat
COM-ÉIS	means	You eat
COM-EN	means	They eat

MODEL – IR VERB

VIV-O	means	I live
VIV-ES	means	You live
VIV-E	means	He / She / It lives
VIV-IMOS	means	We live
VIV-ÍS	means	You live
VIV-EN	means	They live

So, to form **regular verbs** in the **Present Simple** tense, you have to learn the three different sets of **endings** for AR, ER and IR **verbs**, and add them to the **stem**.

Each **ending** will tell us who is doing the action of the **verb**.

This is one of the key differences between Spanish and English in terms of the way in which the languages work. Just take a moment to consider this difference. Look at the following English **regular verb** written out below:

I look at	We look at
You look at	You look at
He / She / It looks at	They look at

Notice how all the parts of the **verb** are the same, except one.
The third one (*he, she, it*) is the only part of a **regular verb** in English that changes, by adding an "s".

In English, it is the word that goes before the **verb** that tells us who is doing the action of the **verb** - e.g. *we* look at, *they* look at.

We and *they* are examples of what we call **subject pronouns**.

Subject pronouns do exist in Spanish. Here they are:

Yo	I
Tú	You
Él	He
Ella	She
Ello	It*
Nosotros	We
Vosostros	You
Ellos / Ellas	They

* Ello is virtually never used – you can forget about it!

So, it is possible in Spanish to say:

Yo miro	I look at

But it is perfectly acceptable to just say miro.
Can you see why?

The reason is that the **endings** are different for each person. Miro can only mean *I* look at. It can't mean anybody else.
If I wanted to say someone else looks at something (not *I*), I wouldn't say miro, I would say one of the other parts of the **verb**.

So the **subject pronouns** are usually unnecessary in Spanish, whereas in English we can't make sense without them.

In English, we always have to put the **subject pronoun** before the **verb** (e.g. *I* look at, or *he* looks at) in order to tell us who is doing the looking (or whatever other action).

But in Spanish, it is the bit we put on the end of the **verb** which tells us who is doing the looking (or whatever other action).

You do, however, need to learn the **subject pronouns**. On some occasions they have to be used, as you will see later on in the course.

You may be wondering why there are two words for *they* – ellos and ellas

The reason is that ellos is the masculine (male) form and ellas is the feminine (female) form. This concept will be fully explained in Module 3 – you don't need to worry about it now.

Look at the **verb** Mirar which has been written out again here. The format of it has been changed to teach you one further point.

SINGULAR	PLURAL
Miro	Miramos
Miras	Miráis
Mira	Miran

The three on the left, under the column singular, all refer to just one person or thing – *I*, *you* and *he / she / it*.

The three on the right are referred to as plural, because they refer to more than one person or thing – *we*, *you* and *they*.

Grammatically, these different parts of the **verb** are often referred to in the following way:

Miro	first person singular	Miramos	first person plural
Miras	second person singular	Miráis	second person plural
Mira	third person singular	Miran	third person plural

Notice that the second person singular refers to *you* (just one person). The second person plural, on the other hand, refers to *you* (two or more people).

I hope that clears up any potential confusion over the two words for *you*!

Now listen to the first track on the first CD.

TRACK 1, CD1

A **regular verb** means a **verb** that follows the pattern that you have studied here in Module 1.

Once you have grasped how the pattern works, you will be able to apply it to new **verbs** as you learn them.

And that's exactly what I am going to ask you to do in your first Practice Activity.

PRACTICE ACTIVITY ONE

Here are six more **regular verbs** in Spanish. Remember, regular means that they have the same **endings** as the three model **verbs** we have just studied and are formed in exactly the same way. There are two **verbs** from each category (two AR, two ER and two IR). Write them out in the **Present Simple** tense.

HABLAR (*to speak*)   BEBER (*to drink*)   ESCRIBIR (*to write*)
TRABAJAR (*to work*)   VENDER (*to sell*)   RECIBIR (*to receive*)

You can find the answers in the Answers Section at the back.

Now listen to the second track on the first CD.

TRACK 2, CD1

THE SPANISH ALPHABET

Although Spanish and English both use the Roman alphabet, there are some differences that are important to point out at this stage. You will see this from the letters of the Spanish alphabet listed below.

It is also time to start thinking about how Spanish and English differ from each other in terms of the sounds of the letters.

Pronunciation is a key area of learning any language, and the sooner you start to form good habits in how you pronounce letters and words in Spanish, the better.

For that reason, most of your work in this Module will involve using the CD.

In this section you will also be learning the meaning of some Spanish words, as an example word is given for each letter of the Spanish alphabet. What follows underneath is exactly that, with the English meanings of the words written in brackets below.

A	alfabeto (alphabet)	B	bien (well)	C	cerca (near)
D	dinero (money)	E	escuchar (to listen to)	F	familia (family)
G	gato (cat)	H	hora (time, hour)	I	imposible (impossible)
J	joven (young)	L	libro (book)	LL	llamar (to call)
M	madre (mother)	N	nunca (never)	Ñ	niño (small boy)

O	opinión (opinion)	P	preguntar (to ask)	Q	querer (to want)
R	regalo (present, gift)	S	ser (to be)	T	tiempo (time, weather)
U	usted (you, *polite*)	V	venir (to come)	Y	yo (I)
Z	zapato (shoe)				

Now listen to the third track on the first CD.

TRACK 3, CD1

So, as you have seen and now heard, there are some differences between the English and Spanish alphabets. Now follows a list of some of the important points regarding Spanish spelling and pronunciation to bear in mind.

- On occasions when in English we use "ph" to make an "f" sound, just an "f" is used in Spanish, as in the example word for the letter "a" – alfabeto. There is no "ph" in Spanish.

- The letter "b" is a subtler, softer sound in Spanish than in English. You will hear this on the CD in a moment.

- The letter "c" is a hard sound (like the English "k") except when it is followed by the letters "e" or "i", when its sound is like "th" in English.

- The letter "g" also has two sounds, sometimes hard like in English (like gato above) and sometimes like the Spanish "j" (a sound difficult to explain in writing!) Like the letter "c", "g" assumes the latter sound when followed by an "e" or an "i".

- The only silent letter in the Spanish alphabet is "h". That means that although it appears at the beginning or in the middle of some words, it is never pronounced. Every other letter in Spanish is always pronounced.
  When you are pronouncing a word that has an "h" in it, you have to imagine it is not there.

- The "ll" – a "double l" – in Spanish is pronounced like a "y". Some dictionaries don't put a separate letter entry in for "ll", as it is thought to be two letters, and so just follow on in the entry for "l". However, there are a substantial number of words that begin with "ll" in Spanish, so I have chosen to introduce it as a separate letter.

- The "ñ" sounds like "n" and "y" together – "ny".

- Many words in Spanish contain "rr". This requires you to roll the tongue.

- The "z" in Spanish is pronounced like a "th", like the "c" when it is followed by an "e" or an "i".

Now listen to the fourth and fifth tracks on the first CD.

TRACK 4 / 5, CD1

Turn back now to the Practice Activity at the end of Module 1, and listen to the sixth track on the first CD.

TRACK 6, CD1

NOUNS AND ARTICLES

NOUN	A person, a place or a thing
DEFINITE ARTICLE	*the* (el, la, los, las)
INDEFINITE ARTICLE	*a / some* (un, una, unos, unas)
MASCULINE	male
FEMININE	female

A **noun** refers to a thing. So a table, a football or a leaf are all examples of **nouns**. A person or a place is also a **noun**.

All **nouns** in Spanish have a gender. That means that they are either **masculine** or **feminine**.

This is a strange concept for English people, because in English there isn't this kind of distinction. Let's consider an example.

We don't think of a table as being inherently male or female, a table is just a table for us – a 'thing' that we call *it*.

But in Spanish (and in several other European languages as well) every 'thing' – be it a table, a swimming pool, a rabbit or whatever – has an inherent gender.

Things (i.e. **nouns**) are either **masculine** or **feminine**.

To go back to our example, the word for table in Spanish is mesa, and it is in fact **feminine**.

This poses a problem for the student of Spanish. In English, when we want to say *the boy* or *the girl* for example, we use the word *the* in both cases. *The* – as stated above – is called in grammar terms the **definite article**.

In Spanish, however, the **definite article** for a **masculine noun** and for a **feminine noun** is different.

The **definite article** for a **masculine noun** is el, for example:

el chico	the boy
el profesor	the teacher

The **definite article** for a **feminine noun** is la, for example:

la chica	the girl
la mesa	the table

You may be wondering how we can know if a **noun** is **masculine** or **feminine**.

The answer is that we cannot know with certainty, and part of learning Spanish involves simply having to remember which **nouns** are **masculine** and which are **feminine**.

It is obvious that the word for man is going to be **masculine**, and the word for woman is going to be **feminine**, but even working along those lines of logic has its limits. For example – and this really is beyond the realm of reason – the word for the male reproductive organ in Spanish is **feminine**, and the word for the female reproductive organ is **masculine**!

However, there are some guidelines that can help you to know the gender of **nouns** that you hear or see written for the first time.

■ If a **noun** ends in the letter "o", it is almost certainly **masculine**.

■ If a **noun** ends in the letter "a", it is almost certainly **feminine**.

(The reason I say "almost certainly" is that there are a handful of exceptions, but they are very few and therefore this is a vital rule to remember).

■ If a **noun** ends in "ción" it is always **feminine**. (The **nouns** that do are invariably the equivalents of words ending "tion" in English, like *station*, *information*, *reputation*.)

The gender of **nouns** that end in other letters can't be known – they must be learnt.

When the **indefinite article** (the word for *a* or *some*) is used in Spanish, the same principle applies. There is a different word for **masculine** and **feminine nouns**.

The **indefinite article** for a **masculine noun** is un, for example:

un gato	a cat
un hombre	a man

The **indefinite article** for a **feminine noun** is una, for example:

una casa	a house
una mujer	a woman

Unfortunately, the differences between Spanish and English don't stop there! There are also different **articles** (**definite** and **indefinite**) depending on whether a **noun** is singular or plural.

Singular means that the **noun** is just one thing, e.g. book.
Plural means that there is more than one, e.g. books.

This concept of singular and plural was touched on in Module 1. Have a look below.

El chico means *the boy*, but if I want to say *the boys* (i.e. more than one), then the word for *the* changes from el to los

Likewise, la mesa means *the table*, but if you want to say *the tables* (i.e. more than one), yet another word for *the* is needed – the word las

With the **indefinite articles** it is the same.

In English, the plural of *a cat* for example, is *some cats*.

The word for *some* when the **noun** is **masculine** is unos
And the word for *some* when the **noun** is **feminine** is unas

This can all seem a bit confusing at first. It is the kind of information that can best be expressed graphically. What you have learnt in this Module is that in Spanish there are:

Four words for the word *the*:   el, la, los, las.

Two words for the word *a*:   un, una.

Two words for the word *some*:   unos, unas.

It will be helpful to express this further in graphical form:

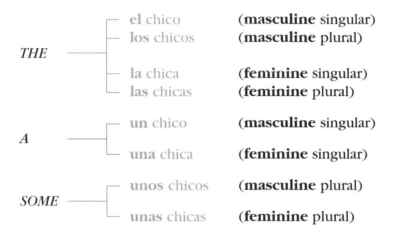

THE
- el chico   (**masculine** singular)
- los chicos   (**masculine** plural)
- la chica   (**feminine** singular)
- las chicas   (**feminine** plural)

A
- un chico   (**masculine** singular)
- una chica   (**feminine** singular)

SOME
- unos chicos   (**masculine** plural)
- unas chicas   (**feminine** plural)

An important point.

Have you noticed that when the **noun** is plural, its form changes? Look how an "s" has been added to the words chico and chica.

This rule applies to all **nouns** that end in a vowel.

However, if a **noun** ends in a consonant, "es" is added to form the plural.

Look at the following examples of this:

el profesor   los profesores

una mujer   unas mujeres

la opinión   las opiniones

un árbol   unos árboles

Now it's time to learn some words. Here follows a list of ten **nouns** which you will need for the Practice Activity that follows.

Don't worry about how to pronounce these words for the moment. The CD activity will help you with that afterwards.

For now, just have a look at the list – you may well know some of the words already.

naranja	orange
plátano	banana
uva	grape
comida	food / meal
verduras	vegetables
pescado	fish
carne	meat
patata	potato
tomate	tomato
cebolla	onion

PRACTICE ACTIVITY TWO

Answer the following questions:

1. How many of these words can you be pretty sure of what gender they are?

2. Which ones can you not be sure of? (In the Answers Section you can see their gender).

3. Take a moment to flick back to Module 2 and the words that you learnt from the alphabet. Pick out all the **nouns** in that list, and decide which gender each one is.

4. Now translate the phrases that follow from Spanish into English. They involve using the ten words you have just read. Be confident, with what you have studied so far you have the necessary tools to complete this activity. Take as much time as you need, and use this Module to refresh your memory and help you with the exercise.

a) las patatas
b) una cebolla
c) un tomate
d) las verduras
e) la naranja
f) los plátanos
g) unos pescados
h) unas patatas
i) la uva
j) las comidas

5. Now have a go at translating the following phrases from English into Spanish:

a) the fish
b) a potato
c) some vegetables
d) the onions
e) the meat
f) some bananas
g) the tomatoes
h) some grapes
i) the meal
j) an orange

You can find the answers in the Answers Section at the back.

Now listen to the seventh track on the first CD.

TRACK 7, CD1

POSSESSIVE ADJECTIVES

4

POSSESSIVE ADJECTIVES	The words that mean *my, your, his, her, its, our, your, their*.

As you will be in the process of realizing, the Spanish language works differently from English.

It's not just a case of learning different words, it's understanding how the language actually works.

What this Module deals with is what we call **possessive adjectives**. They are the words that tell us who something belongs to, i.e. *my* house, *his* car etc.

They present yet another example of how Spanish and English differ from each other.

Let's start by splitting the **possessive adjectives** into two groups – singular and plural.

The reason for doing this will become apparent.

SINGULAR POSSESSIVE ADJECTIVES

Mi / Mis	My
Tu / Tus	Your
Su / Sus	His / Her / Its

They are singular because they are going to describe something that belongs to just <u>one</u> person.

But (and here's where it can get complicated) the singular **possessive adjectives** have a plural form.
Seem strange?

It certainly sounds so at first. But there is a logic to it which is not difficult to understand.

Let's take the first one as an example – mi or mis, both meaning *my*.

There are two forms, depending on whether the thing that belongs to me is singular or plural.

If the thing that belongs to me is a singular thing, I have to use mi.
If the thing that belongs to me is a plural thing, I have to use mis.

mi casa	my house (only one house)
mis casas	my houses (more than one house)

Notice how an "s" is added to the noun when it is plural (i.e. casas). I hope you remember that from the previous Module.

Where native English speakers can get confused is when they start thinking that mi (*my*) is referring to only one person (i.e. me) and so how can there be a plural form?

The golden rule about how these **possessive adjectives** work is that they agree with the noun.

In other words, if the noun is singular, the **possessive adjective** must be singular (i.e. mi) and if the noun is plural, then the **possessive adjective** must be plural (i.e. mis).

Consider again:

mi maleta   *my* suitcase

We are using mi because I've only got one suitcase, *not because I am only one person*.

If I have two or more suitcases, then I have to say:

mis maletas   *my* suitcases

I am still only one person (of course!), but now the thing that is mine (i.e. *my* suitcases) is plural, so mis has to agree with the noun.

If the noun is plural, we have to use mis.

The other singular **possessive adjectives** work in exactly the same way.

Here are some example sentences to demonstrate this:

tu opinión	your opinion
tus regalos	your presents
tu libro	your book
tus primos	your cousins
su gato	his / her cat
sus cebollas	his / her onions
su manzana	his / her apple
sus cosas	his / her things

There are a couple of further points to make with respect to what you have learnt here:

1. In Module 1 you learnt the word tú as a subject pronoun meaning *you*, and now you are learning tu as a **possessive adjective** meaning *your*.

Notice how there is an accent (the slanting line above the "u") on the subject pronoun. That is there simply to differentiate between the two words.

So, if you see tú (with an accent) you know it means *you*.
And if you see tu (without an accent) you know it means *your*.

The use of an accent to distinguish between two words that are spelt and pronounced the same is discussed again in Module 14.

2. With respect to su and sus, you might be wondering how you can tell when they mean *his*, when they mean *her*, and when they mean *its*.

The answer is that you will almost always know from the context. Consider this example situation:

You are talking to someone in Spanish about Pedro (this is the Spanish name for Peter). The person you are talking to is a mutual friend of both Peter and you.

In the course of the conversation you say, "su coche". Because of the context of your conversation – which is about Pedro – it's pretty clear that su coche means "*his car*", i.e. Pedro's car. Usually it will be obvious from the context who su is referring to.

If it isn't obvious, then it might be necessary to specify whose car (or whatever the noun is) you are talking about. This is easy to do.

Consider the potentially confusing situation below:

You are talking to someone in Spanish again, but this time you are talking about Pedro and his sister Alicia (Alice). Both of them have cats, and in the course of the conversation one of you says, "su gato". It would depend on what had just been said prior to that, but there could conceivably be some confusion as to whose cat was being talked about. Su gato might mean Pedro's cat (*his cat*) or Alicia's cat (*her cat*).

So, to remove that confusion, we would have to say, "Pedro's cat" or "Alicia's cat".

But (and this won't surprise you by now!) the structure in Spanish to express this is different from in English.

In English, when we want to say that something belongs to someone, we use an apostrophe + "s". Like this:

> Simon's book
> Richard's apples

In Spanish, there is no apostrophe.

What we have to say literally is "the book of Simon", or "the apples of Richard".

The Spanish word for *of* is de

So, we say it like this:

> Simon's book   el libro de Simon
> Richard's apples   las manzanas de Richard

If I want to specify that I mean *his car* instead of *her car* for example, all I have to do is use the subject pronouns él and ella

| his house | la casa de él |
| her shoes | los zapatos de ella |

Bear in mind that él and ella mean *he* and *she*, but when used in the way shown here are translated as *his* and *her*.

Have a look back at Module 1 if you need to remind yourself about the subject pronouns.

Let's take a moment to practice what you have just learnt.

Understanding the theory of something is only the first part. To grasp any concept properly – to cement it well and truly – you must put it into immediate practice.

PRACTICE ACTIVITY THREE

1. Translate the following into English:

    a) las patatas de Roberto
    b) el libro de María
    c) la familia de Miguel
    d) los zapatos de Ana
    e) el dinero de Ricardo
    f) la tienda de Carlos
    g) los estudiantes de ella

2. Translate the following into Spanish (I will keep using Spanish names so that you continue to get used to seeing and using them):

    a) Manuel's house
    b) Juan's books
    c) Alberto's onions
    d) Elena's oranges
    e) Alicia's teacher
    f) Miguel's friends
    g) Rosa's computer

Check your answers in the Answers Section.

Now let's have a look at the plural **possessive adjectives**.
These are the words that mean *our*, *your* and *their*.

They are the same as the singular ones in that they have to agree with the noun.

In other words, there is a different form depending on whether the noun is singular or plural.

However, with the first two (*our* and *your*), as well as there being a singular and plural form, there are also different forms depending on whether the noun is masculine or feminine.

So, there are four forms in all.

This sounds confusing, and indeed it is without any examples.
Don't worry, you will understand in a minute.

Have a look, then, at the plural **possessive adjectives**:

PLURAL POSSESSIVE ADJECTIVES

Nuestro / Nuestra / Nuestros / Nuestras	Our
Vuestro / Vuestra / Vuestros / Vuestras	Your
Su / Sus	Their

For the moment, don't worry about su and sus.

You can see that with the *our* and *your* **possessive adjectives** there are four forms, which are:

Masculine singular, feminine singular, masculine plural and feminine plural.

Remember, **possessive adjectives** agree with the nouns they refer to.

So, whether the noun is masculine or feminine and singular or plural will determine which form of the **possessive adjective** you have to use.

Look at the following examples:

nuestro libro	our book (nuestro is for masculine singular nouns)
nuestra madre	our mother (nuestra is for feminine singular nouns)
nuestros libros	our books (nuestros is for masculine plural nouns)
nuestras madres	our mothers (nuestras is for feminine plural nouns)

Vuestro works in exactly the same way:

vuestro padre   your father (vuestro is for masculine singular nouns)

vuestra familia   your family (vuestra is for feminine singular nouns)

vuestros perros   your dogs (vuestros is for masculine plural nouns)

vuestras familias   your families (vuestras is for feminine plural nouns)

You are probably surprised to see that su and sus – as well as meaning *his*, *her* and *its* – also mean *their*.

su opinión   their opinion

sus hijos   their children

This can be confusing at times.

But usually you will know from the context who su is referring to.

And when it's not clear, you have already learnt how to avoid potential confusion through the exercises you have just done in Practice Activity Three.

Now listen to the eighth track on the first CD.

TRACK 8, CD1

While things are still fresh in your mind, do the next Practice Activity which shouldn't take you long. Always use your notes to help you do the Practice Activities if you need to. I would be very surprised if you didn't need them – that could be the sign that you are a genius!

PRACTICE ACTIVITY FOUR

1. Translate into English:

a) nuestras vidas

b) su cerveza*

c) mi reloj

d) el coche de mi hermano

e) vuestra hermana

f) tus ideas

g) el trabajo de él

h) su coche*

i) vuestros miembros

j) sus amigos*

* Remember that **su** can refer to different people.

2. Translate into Spanish:

a) his money

b) our land

c) their sisters

d) my friend

e) your presents

f) your (plural) parents

g) our grapes

h) her hopes

i) your breakfast

j) my cherries

Check your answers in the Answers Section.

You have now reached your first Progress Check in the course. There are four in total, one after every four Modules.

The purpose of the Progress Checks is simply to provide you with more practice exercises, so that you can see how well you are doing. If you can do the exercises without referring to your notes, then of course it's better. But if you can't remember certain points, or want to be absolutely sure, then use the course to refresh your memory.

It is only through practice that you can cement your understanding. You will need a dictionary to look up some words. Apart from that, all the knowledge you need has been covered in what you have studied so far.

The Progress Checks will get you to link the things that you have studied in the different Modules. So, in the sentences you will be asked to translate, you will have to put together the things you learnt in each Module. These exercises can be repeated again and again, so use them as you see fit.

For example, you might want to try them right now, without any revision of the first four Modules, just to test how much you remember. Then you could try them again in a few days, after revising the parts that you got wrong (if you do get anything wrong, of course!)

Alternatively, you could treat the exercises as an exam and revise first before looking at the questions. Then you can try the exercises when you feel ready.

The method is up to you, because you are studying alone. Different methods will suit different people. The only thing I would say is try to use the Progress Checks to your advantage. Be honest with yourself about the method that will suit you best. Treat them as a vital part of the course. Your results will show you exactly how well you have understood the material, and give you the opportunity to practise, which is the only way you will really absorb and remember what you have learnt.

Never underestimate the importance of practice, practice, practice. If you don't practise, you will forget about 90% of everything you study in this course within a year. That is the harsh reality of a human being's powers of retention!

So, when you are ready, have a go at the following exercises. You can find the answers as always in the Answers Section.

PART ONE

Write out the following regular verbs in the Present Simple Tense:

1. Cantar (to sing)

2. Responder (to answer, respond)

3. Subir (to go up, climb)

PART TWO

Translate the following sentences into English:

1. Cantan en el autobús.*

2. Bebes mi vino.

3. Las uvas de María.

4. Su hermano sube la montaña.*1

5. Miramos los juguetes de los niños.

6. Nuestro gato come pescado.

7. Su madre cocina las verduras.*1 & *2

8. Recibimos un regalo de nuestra abuela.*3

9. El profesor bebe té con whisky en la clase.

10. Coméis unos tomates.

    *   **en** is the Spanish word for *in* or *on*.
    *1 There is more than one possible translation of this sentence because we don't know who **su** is referring to.
    *2 **cocina** comes from the verb **cocinar**, which means *to cook*.
    *3 You learnt in Module 4 that **de** means *of*. **De** also means *from*, which you will probably see from this sentence is how it should be translated here.

PART THREE

Translate the following sentences into Spanish:

1. They drink coffee.

2. I eat my oranges.

3. The little boy writes a letter.

4. Our friends live in London.*

5. We work in Spain.*

6. My sister sells her house.

7. The mothers buy fish.

8. Your friend eats some grapes.

9. In Juan's house they eat meat.*1

10. I look at the cats.*2

11. We drink some beers in the garden.*

12. The teacher writes on the blackboard.*

13. The man in the house eats some tomatoes.*

14. My wife prepares dinner.*3

15. You (plural) speak Italian.

16. Your father eats garlic.

17. My sister's friend cooks rice.*4

18. I eat your (plural) cherries.

19. Their cousins receive some letters from her uncle.*5

20. My friend's wife drinks the wine and eats some onions and a potato.*6 *7

*   **en** is the Spanish word for *in* or *on*.

*1 *In the house of Juan.*

*2 Because in this sentence **mirar** is followed by a personal thing (i.e. cats) as opposed to just an object, the personal "**a**" is used after **mirar**. In other words, in this sentence, you have to put the word "**a**" (meaning *to* or *at*) after the verb **mirar**. The personal "**a**" is dealt with in Module 16.

*3 In Spanish, the name of a meal (breakfast, lunch or dinner) is always preceded by the definite article. In other words, they always say "the breakfast", "the lunch" and "the dinner".

*4 *The friend of my sister*.

*5 **de** means *of* or *from*.

*6 *The wife of my friend*.

*7 The Spanish word for *and* is **y** (pronounced "ee")

PART FOUR

In the following sentences, change the infinitive (in brackets) to the correct part of the verb and translate the sentences. The subject pronouns are given to tell you which part of the verb you should change the infinitive to. Look back to Module 1 to remind yourself of the subject pronouns if you need to. See the example.

e.g.   Ella (beber) vino.
      Ella bebe vino.   She drinks wine.

1.   Nosotros (hablar) español.

2.   Yo (trabajar) en Valencia.

3.   Vosotros (vivir) en el centro.

4.   Su primo (escribir) muchos artículos.*

5.   Tus padres (comer) carne.

6.   Mi padre (cocinar) por la noche.*1

7.   Nosotros (responder) a las preguntas de la profesora.

8.   Tú (beber) soda con tu whisky.

9.   Mis abuelos (recibir) flores de unos amigos en Francia.

10. Él (hablar) italiano.

11. Ellos (cantar) una canción.

12. Ellos (recibir) nuestros regalos.

13. Mi hermana (vender) su coche.

14. Vosotros (cantar) en la iglesia.*2

15. Tú (vivir) con tu abuela.

    *   **muchos** means *many / a lot of*.

    *1 **por la noche** means *at night*.

    *2 This sentence translates better into English without the article (i.e. *church*, instead of *the church*).

IRREGULAR VERBS

KEY GRAMMAR TERMS

IRREGULAR VERBS	Verbs which do not follow the normal pattern studied in Module 1.
REGULAR VERBS	Verbs which follow the normal pattern.
SER / ESTAR	The two verbs in Spanish that mean *to be*.
TENER	The verb *to have*

In every language there are **irregular verbs**. They refer to verbs which do not follow the 'regular' pattern – in Spanish, that means the pattern you studied in the first Module.

The unfortunate thing is that **irregular verbs** are always the most common verbs – the ones that we use most frequently.
So it's necessary to learn them early on in the study of a language.

We are going to look at three **irregular verbs** in this Module.

Consider English for a moment. In Module 1 we looked at an example of how a **regular** English **verb** goes in the Present Simple tense.

We looked at the verb *to take*. Here it is again:

I take	We take
You take	You take
He / She / It takes	They take

You will probably remember that it was pointed out that the only ending that is different in the present tense of a **regular verb** in English is the ending for *he*, *she* and *it*, when we add an "s" - *takes* instead of *take*.

That's why in English we always have to put the subject pronouns in front – *I, you, he, she, it, we, you* and *they* – so that we know who it is that is doing the action of the verb.

Now have a look at an **irregular** English **verb** - the verb *to be*. This is the most important and frequently used verb in any language.

I am	We are
You are	You are
He / She / It is	They are

Notice how it is different from a **regular verb**. There are three different words that are used – *am*, *are* and *is*.
The word *be* does not appear in the conjugation of the verb at all. We don't say:

I be, you be etc, as we would if it was a **regular verb**.

It is formed in a different way. So it is called an **irregular verb**.

In Module 1 you saw how the endings for each part of the verb are all different in Spanish.

That's why we can nearly always omit the subject pronouns, because we know from the ending who is doing the action of the verb.

That's true for any kind of **verb** in Spanish - **regular** or **irregular**.

It is a shame in many ways that it's necessary to study the **irregular verbs** so soon, but unfortunately it is.

The reason for this, as I have already said, is that 90% of **irregular verbs** are extremely common - the words that we use most often in everyday speech.

So when you are speaking Spanish to someone, they are the verbs that you are going to be hearing and using more than others.

You would be incredibly limited in what you can say in Spanish without the three **irregular verbs** that we are going to study in this Module.

We can't wait any longer! Even though you've only just got used to the way **regular verbs** work, it's already time to probe deeper and consider 'abnormal' (**irregular**) **verbs**.

But don't worry or be overawed. Our approach will be systematic as always.

Firstly, it's helpful to think that there are three ways in which a **verb** can be **irregular**.

Think back for a moment to Module 1, and the meaning of the infinitive.

That's the bit of the verb that ends in "ar", "er" or "ir" and means *to do* something (e.g. *to take*, *to eat*, *to write*).

We split the infinitive into its two parts – the stem and the ending – in order to form the Present Simple tense.
I hope this makes sense. Have a look back to Module 1 if you need reminding.

An **irregular verb** can be irregular in the following three ways:

- The stem can change
- The endings can change (i.e. be different from the regular endings)
- Both the stem and the endings can change

As you learn the **irregular verbs** – little by little of course - you will see how this is true.

Let's start with *to be*. In Spanish, that means learning two verbs, because there are two words that mean *to be*.
Yet another strange concept for the English mind. You must be getting used to it by now!

Let's look at the pattern of the two verbs first, and then we'll consider why there are two verbs in Spanish for the one in English, and what the differences are between them.

SER (*to be*)	ESTAR (*to be*)
Soy	Estoy
Eres	Estás
Es	Está
Somos	Estamos
Sois	Estáis
Son	Están

The first one may strike you as being more irregular than the second one. In fact, estar (an AR verb) only differs from mirar (our model AR verb from Module 1) in the first person – estoy.

After that it follows the normal, regular pattern. However, it only needs the slightest deviation from the regular pattern to be classed as irregular.

So, soy and estoy both mean *I am*, and eres and estás both mean *you are*, etc.

Have a look below:

Soy / Estoy	I am
Eres / Estás	You are
Es / Está	He / She / It is
Somos / Estamos	We are
Sois / Estáis	You are
Son / Están	They are

It is strange at first to think of there being two verbs meaning *to be*.

So, what is the difference between saying one and saying the other? Are they the same? Why are there two verbs in Spanish for the one in English?

The answer, as you have probably guessed by now, is that they are not the same. There are rules about when you have to use one and when the other.

There is one basic guideline about when to use ser and when to use estar.

■ Ser is used for permanent things.

Soy inglés.	I am English. (I will always be English.)
Son mis padres.	They are my parents. (Nothing can ever change that.)

■ Estar is used for temporary things.

Estoy feliz.	I am happy. (Right now, but I don't know about later.)
Estamos en la cocina.	We are in the kitchen. (at the moment)

Ser expresses facts of an unchangeable nature.
Estar expresses something that is true, but only at the moment.

However, there are exceptions to these rules.
This is not an easy thing in Spanish.

The difference between ser and estar is an area of Spanish grammar that does cause students a headache or two.

Consider these four sentences in English, and think about which verb (ser or estar) you would need to use in Spanish if you were going to translate them.

1. My friend *is* angry with his parents.
2. I *am* not from here, so I don't know the custom about tipping.
3. My mum *is* waiting for me.
4. Where *are* you?

Only one of the sentences would use ser (the permanent verb) in Spanish. Which one?

I hope you can see that the answer is the second one.

In the other three sentences, we would have to use the verb estar because they each express a temporary situation, as opposed to an unchanging fact.

However, it is not quite as simple as that.

The rules that you have just learnt are basic guidelines that will serve you well most of the time.
But as has been stated, there are also some exceptions to the rules, and some other concepts that you need to understand.

Another key use of estar is to talk about position or location. Usually this is temporary anyway, so there is no conflict of rules. Consider the following sentence:

Estamos en la oficina.   We are in the office. (our current location)

Presumably I am not going to stay in the office for the rest of my life! That is clearly a temporary thing.

But, if I want to say that London is in England, I am talking about a location (i.e. where London is) but I am also saying something that is permanent by nature. (i.e. London will always be in England.)

So there is a conflict of the rules we have learnt. The correct sentence in Spanish in this case is:

Londres está en Inglaterra.

So, remember that estar is used to talk about position and location, even when that describes a permanent fact.

There are some further exceptions to the basic rule you have learnt.

It is only worth considering a couple of these exceptions now, because some of the cases are rather obscure. Consider these two:

1.   Ser is used whenever we talk about professions, or being a student.

e.g.   Es médico.   He is a doctor.
       Son profesores.   They are teachers.
       Somos estudiantes.   We are students.

In the first two sentences, even though the person / people might change their profession in the future, we still have to use the permanent verb.

It is totally wrong to use estar when we are talking about professions.

And in the third sentence, it is certain that we will not always be students, and yet you have to use the permanent verb, ser.

These are rules that just have to be learnt.

Notice another thing here. The indefinite article (the word meaning *a*) is left out when we talk about professions in Spanish.

In English, we have to say *he is a doctor*, but in Spanish literally we just say "he is doctor", without the article.

Notice also how the noun becomes plural when the subject (the person or people) is plural. This is the same as in English.

       Soy abogado.   I am a lawyer.
       Somos abogados. (add an "s") We are lawyers.

Refer back to Module 3 if you need to revise how to make a noun plural.

2.   Estar is used when we say *to be married*.

       estar casado   to be married

This is not a reflection of Spanish cynicism regarding the permanency of marriage!
It is just another rule that you have to remember.

       Estoy casado.   I am married.

If it was a woman talking, she would have to say:

> **Estoy** casada.   I am married.

The "o" changes to an "a" when the sentence refers to a woman.

In the next Module you will be looking at adjectives, where this will be explained in more detail.

So, keep in mind this general rule that ser is used for permanent things and estar is used to talk about location / position and temporary things.

One further point.

One of the examples given above with estar was the following:

> **Estoy** feliz.   I am happy.

However, it is also possible to say:

> **Soy** feliz.   I am happy.

Although the sentences are translated the same in English, the meaning of them is different.

Estoy feliz means I am happy now, because of a particular reason. Perhaps I just won some money, or passed an exam or found a girlfriend. In other words, my happiness is related to my circumstances.
It is the temporary verb we are using (estar), so it means my feeling is also temporary.

Soy feliz is referring to my basic personality – I am a happy person by nature. To express this idea, we need to use the permanent verb – ser.

This can apply to many things. Let's take one more example, and that should be enough for you to get the idea.

> **Estás** guapo / guapa.   You are beautiful / good-looking.
> **Eres** guapo / guapa.   You are beautiful / good-looking.

The first one is a common compliment to give someone in Spanish. It is used when someone has made an effort to look nice, perhaps by dressing up and / or wearing make up. But it has nothing to do with someone's natural looks.

It could be said to the plainest person in the world!

The second one uses the permanent verb (ser) and refers to someone's natural appearance. It is used to describe someone who is generally thought to be attractive or good-looking.

Let's take time to practise a little of what you have learnt so far about ser and estar.

PRACTICE ACTIVITY FIVE

1. Translate the following sentences from Spanish into English:

    a) Somos profesores.
    b) El gato está debajo de la mesa.
    c) Estamos cerca de la playa.*
    d) Sois de Italia.
    e) Manuel es mi amigo.
    f) Estoy en la cocina con mi novia.
    g) Nuestros padres están en España.

    > * **cerca**, as you studied in Module 2, means *near*. If a noun follows the word **cerca**, you have to put the word **de** – meaning *of* or *from* – in between them. This is explained more clearly in Module 16, so don't worry about it now.

2. Now have a go at translating from English into Spanish (more difficult, but be confident!):

    a) His parents are teachers.
    b) My sister is in the garden.
    c) You (plural) are in the house.
    d) I am a student.
    e) Your friends are from England.
    f) Your friends are in England.
    g) Our cousin (female) is married.

Check your answers in the Answers Section.

Before reflecting on what you have learnt in this Module with the CD, we need to look at one other **irregular verb** first, and that is the verb tener, which means *to have*.

Actually, just as there are two verbs for *to be* in Spanish, there are also two verbs for *to have*, but we only need to concentrate on one of them in this course.

Tener means *to have* in the sense of possession.

In other words, it is used when we are talking about something that belongs to someone.

Look at these examples:

I *have* a car.
Manuel *has* a cat.
Your parents *have* a lovely house.

In each sentence, the sense of *to have* is a sense of belonging, of possession. Tener is used when it is this meaning of *have* that we want to express.

Here it is in the Present tense.

Tengo
Tienes
Tiene
Tenemos
Tenéis
Tienen

What is irregular about it?

I hope you can see that the stem is irregular in three of the six parts. The first person singular is a bit strange as well, isn't it?

Tener is what we can call a 'Boot Verb', which is a term that will be covered in detail in Module 10, but it's useful to explain briefly how boot verbs work at this point.

First of all, I am going to write out the verb in two columns, singular and plural.

Tengo	Tenemos
Tienes	Tenéis
Tiene	Tienen

Boot verbs are **verbs** which are **irregular** because the stem changes. However, the stem change doesn't run throughout the whole verb. In which three parts of tener does the stem change?

I hope you were able to see that it changes in the second and third person singular (tienes and tiene) and in the third person plural (tienen).

The "e" from the original stem changes to an "ie".

So why are they called boot verbs? Look below, and see how I have drawn a boot shape around the parts of the verb where the change in the stem occurs.

Tengo	Tenemos
Tienes	Tenéis
Tiene	Tienen

The stem changes from an "e" to an "ie".

There are many verbs which change in this way. You will see this later on in Module 10.

Now here comes a really important point.

Do you remember what the indefinite article is? It was covered in Module 3.

It means the words that mean *a* and *some*.
They are un, una, unos and unas.
Look back if you want to remind yourself.

In colloquial Spanish, the indefinite article after tener is often dropped.

In English, for example, we say:

I have a car.

You would think that that would be translated into Spanish like this:

Tengo un coche.

But in typical spoken Spanish, people tend to say (but not always) just:

Tengo coche. (without the un)

In written Spanish, however, the article should always be used.

Don't be surprised then, when you hear spoken Spanish, that the indefinite article is often omitted after tener.

After learning something new, it is always important to put it into immediate practice. That is the only way that you can become confident – by using what you learn so many times that it becomes natural to you.

Throughout this course there are many exercises which are designed to cement your knowledge. With this in mind, try the next Practice Activity in which you will have to use the different parts of tener

PRACTICE ACTIVITY SIX

5

1.   Translate the following phrases into Spanish:

a) My father has two sisters.
b) I have a cat.
c) Your parents have a flat in Italy.
d) We have some oranges.
e) His mother has three friends.
f) You (plural) have a car.
g) You have one daughter.*

  * In this sentence, you must put the article because it means "one" not "a".

Check your answers in the Answers Section.

Now listen to the ninth track on the first CD.

TRACK 9, CD1

ADJECTIVES

ADJECTIVES   Words that describe nouns.

Adjectives are words used to describe things (nouns).

If you asked a hundred people to imagine a table, each person would imagine something different. But if they were asked to imagine a small, round, glass table, they would all imagine something similar.

The words "small", "round" and "glass" describe what the table is like. They are **adjectives**.

In order to get you used to identifying different words, do the following brief exercise.

PRACTICE ACTIVITY SEVEN

Look at the following sentences in English and pick out all the **adjectives** there are.

Remember, you are looking for words which describe something or someone.

1.   The man in the black coat was carrying a small umbrella under his arm.

2.   There was an old oak door which creaked as the unshaven jailor pushed it slowly open.

3.   Opening the coarse brown envelope which contained her exam results
      was a tense moment for everyone.

Check your answers in the Answers Section.

Hopefully, it's now clear to you what **adjectives** are, and you can identify them in sentences.

Now let's learn some **adjectives** in Spanish.

Later in the Module we will consider some rules about **adjectives**, but for now, let's list some useful ones. Some of them you will have come across in the course already.

inglés	English
español	Spanish
grande	big*
pequeño	small*
feliz	happy
triste	sad
loco	mad
rico	rich
pobre	poor*
cómodo	comfortable
nuevo	new*
bueno	good*
malo	bad*
gordo	fat
delgado	thin / slim
guapo	handsome / pretty
enfadado	angry
fácil	easy
difícil	difficult
famoso	famous

The **adjectives** marked with an asterix all have peculiarities about them (six in all). They are all very common words, and need special attention.

We will look at them each individually in the second part of this Module.

Let's list the other fourteen **adjectives** again, this time in a different order. Cover up the translation, and see how many meanings you can remember.

Probably you will surprise yourself. A lot of the words are similar to the English word. I would hazard a guess that you will remember most of them.

gordo	fat
triste	sad
inglés	English
guapo	beautiful / good-looking
difícil	difficult
delgado	thin / slim
rico	rich
español	Spanish
enfadado	angry
feliz	happy
cómodo	comfortable
loco	mad
famoso	famous
fácil	easy

There are two important things about **adjectives** in Spanish which are different from in English:

1. Usually in Spanish, the position of the **adjective** and the noun in a sentence is opposite to English.

Whereas in English it is correct to say *the sad man*, in Spanish you have to say "the man sad."

In English, the **adjective** goes before the noun.
In Spanish, the noun goes before the **adjective**.

This is usually the case. There are some exceptions, and you will see some of them later.

Here are some examples of the **adjective** going after the noun:

Es un hombre famoso.	He is a famous man.
Es un libro inglés.	It's an English book.
Es una chica guapa.	She is a beautiful girl.
Japón es un país rico.	Japan is a rich country.
Es un examen difícil.	It's a difficult exam.

Can you see how in each sentence the word order is different to English?

The **adjectives** (the words describing the nouns) are going after the nouns instead of before them.

2.   **Adjectives** in Spanish have to agree with the nouns they describe.

That means that they change form, depending on whether the nouns they are describing are masculine or feminine, singular or plural.

Unfortunately for the student of Spanish, there are different categories of **adjectives**.

Some agree in number (i.e. singular or plural) and gender (i.e. masculine or feminine). In other words, they have four forms.

But some only agree in number, and don't bother about having a form that distinguishes between masculine and feminine. So they have only two forms.

Does that make sense?

If not, don't worry. This Module will contain a lot of examples to demonstrate the different types of **adjectives** that there are.

Here follows a list of the key rules for making **adjectives** agree in Spanish:

1.   **Adjectives** ending in "o" change to "a" if the noun they describe is feminine singular, "os" if the noun is masculine plural, and "as" if the noun is feminine plural.

In our list of fourteen **adjectives**, there are eight that end in "o".

They are: gordo, rico, enfadado, cómodo, guapo, delgado, famoso and loco.

Here are some examples of how the **adjectives** have to agree with the nouns they describe:

   a) los chicos gordos   the fat boys

The noun is masculine plural, so the **adjective** must take its masculine plural form as well, in order to agree in gender and number.

   b) una mujer famosa   a famous woman

Here the noun is feminine singular, so the **adjective** must take the same form.

   c) Son las familias ricas de Madrid.   They are the rich families of Madrid.

Here the noun is feminine plural, so the **adjective** must be in its feminine plural form also.

d) Mi hermano está enfadado.   My brother is angry.

And lastly, here the noun is masculine singular, so the **adjective** is too.

Here are some more examples with the other words from our list:

El coche es muy cómodo.   The car is very comfortable.
Sus amigos están locos.   His friends are crazy.
Mis hijas son muy guapas.   My daughters are very beautiful.
Eres muy delgada.   You are very slim.*

* In the last sentence, the person being spoken to must be a woman. If it were
  a man, we would have to say delgado.

So that is an interesting point in Spanish.

If I say in English, *you are slim / thin* we can't know just from the words
whether the sentence is addressed to a man or a woman. But in Spanish we
know from the form of the **adjective** that is used.

2.   **Adjectives** ending in "e" don't distinguish between masculine and
      feminine, and add an "s" when they describe plural nouns. Look at these
      examples:

a) Mi hermano está triste.   My brother is sad.
b) Mi hermana está triste.   My sister is sad.

In the first sentence, the noun is masculine (my brother) and in the second
sentence, the noun is feminine (my sister).

But because the **adjective** ends in "e", it doesn't change its form for singular
nouns.
Its form is the same whether the noun is masculine or feminine.

c) Mis hermanos están tristes.   My siblings (i.e. they) are sad.

Here the noun is plural, so the plural form is used – an "s" is added.

3.   **Adjectives** ending in a consonant usually don't distinguish between
      masculine and feminine either, and add an "es" to form the plural.

However, in our list we have two **adjectives** that don't follow this rule.

They are the words inglés and español.

They are called **adjectives** of nationality. There is a separate note about them which you will read in a moment.

There are other **adjectives** which don't follow this rule either, but we will not be looking at them now.

There are three other words in our list (apart from inglés and español) which end in a consonant.

They are: fácil, difícil and feliz.

Feliz needs a separate note as well (see underneath).

Consider these examples with fácil and difícil:

a) Es un examen fácil / difícil.   It's an easy / difficult exam.

b) Mi tarea es fácil / difícil.   My task is easy / difficult.

c) Son palabras difíciles.   They are difficult words.

d) Las clases son fáciles.   The lessons are easy.

Notice how there are only two forms of the **adjective**.

One is singular, and the other is plural (formed by adding "es").

There is no distinction between masculine and feminine.

NB1. inglés and español are **adjectives** of nationality.

In spite of the fact that they end in a consonant, they do have a feminine form.

So, there are four forms in all for each word:

Soy inglés / español.
I am English / Spanish. (referring to a male)

Soy inglesa / española.
I am English / Spanish. (referring to a female)

Somos ingleses / españoles.
We are English / Spanish. (referring to two or more males or a mixed group)

Somos inglesas / españolas.
We are English / Spanish. (referring to two or more females only)

Notice that, unlike in English, they are not written with a capital letter.

NB2. feliz (and all **adjectives** ending in "z") have a special rule to form the plural.

The "z" changes to "c", and then you add "es".

Soy feliz.   I am happy.

Somos felices.   We are happy.

There are more rules about **adjectives** that I have not included here.

The reason is simple: I don't want to overload your mind with information.

There is no point in doing that.

Adjectives are a big subject in Spanish. This Module is an introduction to the most important ones, rather than an exhaustive study of them.

The key points about **adjectives** you have covered here, and it's enough for you to chew over for the moment.

The other rules are not important for you yet.

We still have to look at the other six **adjectives** in our original list. Now could be a good time to take a break if you feel that your mind is overloaded.

Unless you are feeling extremely confident, take a break and tackle the rest of this Module another day. We've actually covered quite a lot of ground in a short time.

So, we are left with the following six **adjectives**: bueno, malo, pobre, nuevo, grande and pequeño.

They are six of the most important **adjectives** that there are in Spanish.

They all have their own peculiarities, but they all have one thing in common and it is this:

Sometimes they are placed before the noun instead of after it.

I have chosen to treat each one individually so that you get to see many example sentences with them in.

Hopefully that will stand you in good stead for the Practice Activity which follows.

BUENO

Bueno is one of a few **adjectives** that can be placed either before or after the noun.
However, if it goes before a masculine noun, it is shortened to buen.

Consider:

Es (un) buen profesor.	He is a good teacher.
Also possible: Es un profesor bueno.	

Although both sentences are grammatically correct, the first one is more usual. If you use the second sentence structure, you must include the article (in this case un).

Es (una) buena enfermera.	She is a good nurse.
Also possible: Es una enfermera buena.	

Tenemos buenos clientes.	We've got good clients.
Also possible: Tenemos clientes buenos.	

Hay* buenas cosas en mi trabajo.	There are good things in my job.
Also possible: Hay cosas buenas en mi trabajo.	

* Hay is a **very** important word in Spanish.
   It means *there is* or *there are*.

MALO

Malo **can also go before or after the noun. It shortens to** mal **when it goes before a masculine noun.**

Tengo un mal profesor de francés.	I've got a bad French teacher.
Also possible: Tengo un profesor malo de francés.	

Mi amiga tiene mala fama.	My friend has a bad reputation.
Also possible (but **not used much**):	Mi amiga tiene una fama mala.

Somos malos estudiantes.	We are bad students.
Also possible: Somos estudiantes malos.	

Son malas razones.	They are bad reasons.
Also possible: Son razones malas.	

POBRE

As it ends in "e", it has only two forms. Pobre can also go before the noun, but when it does the meaning changes.

It is not the same to say el pobre hombre as it is to say el hombre pobre.

El pobre hombre means poor because something bad has happened to him – "poor him!"

El hombre pobre means poor as in "not rich".

Consider these examples:

La gente pobre en Brasil.	The poor (not rich) people in Brazil.
Mi pobre amigo está en el hospital.	My poor friend is in hospital.
Los pobres huérfanos de Nicaragua.	The poor orphans of Nicaragua.
Las zonas pobres de la ciudad.	The poor areas of the city.

NUEVO

Nuevo has four forms. The position of nuevo can go either before or after the noun.

Tengo (un) nuevo coche.   I have a new car.
Also possible: Tengo (un) coche nuevo.

Hay una nueva cocinera en el colegio.   There is a new cook in the school.
Also possible: Hay una cocinera nueva en el colegio.

Son alumnos nuevos.   They are new students.
Also possible: Son nuevos alumnos.

Tenemos instrucciones nuevas.   We have new instructions.
Also possible: Tenemos nuevas instrucciones.

GRANDE

When grande goes before a masculine or feminine noun, it changes its form and becomes gran.

But the meaning of gran is not *big*, but *great*. The form changes and the meaning changes.

Look at these examples:

Es una ciudad grande.	It's a big city.
Es una gran ciudad.	It's a great city.
Tengo un gran amigo.	I have a great friend.
Hay un árbol grande en mi jardín.	There's a big tree in my garden.
Son manzanas grandes.	They are big apples.
Mis amigos tienen coches grandes.	My friends have big cars.

PEQUEÑO

With pequeño, although it is grammatically correct to put the **adjective** before the noun, people very seldom do so. That's why in the following examples pequeño goes after the noun:

Tengo un coche pequeño.	I have a small car.
Viven en una casa pequeña.	They live in a small house.
Tenemos dos perros pequeños.	We have a couple of small dogs.
Son raciones pequeñas de calamares.	They are small portions of squid.

However, in the following sentence, it is impossible to put the **adjective** before the noun. It must go first, as in English.

Tengo un pequeño problema.

The word pequeño is also used to describe a younger sibling, for example:

Tengo una hermana pequeña.	I have a younger sister.
Es mi hermano pequeño.	He is my younger brother.

Now listen to the tenth track on the first CD.

TRACK 10, CD1

1.	Translate the following sentences from Spanish to English:

a)	Somos españoles y vivimos en Salamanca.
b)	Mi padre está enfadado con mi madre porque la casa está sucia.*
c)	Hay muchas familias pobres que viven en Brasil.
d)	Los exámenes de historia no son fáciles.
e)	Tengo una nueva novia.
f)	Estamos en una situación muy difícil.
g)	En nuestra casa tenemos un cuadro famoso de Picasso.
h)	Hay dos chicas muy delgadas en mi clase.
i)	Mi hermano tiene un amigo muy malo.
j)	El novio de mi hermana es muy guapo.

	* **porque**, written as one word, means *because*.

2.	Now try translating from English into Spanish:

a)	My father's boss is a rich man.
b)	It's an English film.
c)	Your teacher has a fat dog.
d)	Barcelona against Real Madrid is a great game.*
e)	His mother is very happy today.
f)	The teacher (female) is not very good.
g)	You (plural) have a small house.
h)	There is a small problem with the car.
i)	The ugly boy sings in the shower.
j)	Your friend's story is very sad.

	* *against* is **contra**.

Check your answers in the Answers Section.

QUESTIONS AND NEGATIVES

AFFIRMATIVE SENTENCE	An affirmation of something (a positive sentence)
NEGATIVE SENTENCE	The opposite of an affirmative sentence
QUESTION SENTENCE	A sentence that asks a question.
INTONATION	The variation of pitch in someone's voice
QUESTION WORDS	Words that typically start a question.

7

In this Module we will study about how to change **affirmative sentences** into **question** and **negative sentences**.

This is wonderfully easy in Spanish compared to in English.

After the difficulties of the last Module (adjectives are not an easy part of Spanish grammar!), this Module will come as a welcome breather.

First of all, just to make things absolutely clear, let me give an example (in English) of each of the sentence types above:

He is going to the cinema tonight.   (an **affirmative sentence**)
He is not going to the cinema tonight. (a **negative sentence**)
Is he going to the cinema tonight?   (a **question sentence**)

QUESTION SENTENCES

Look at the following two sentences in English.

> He is English.
> Is he English?

Notice how the word order changes in English when we want to change an **affirmative sentence** into a **question sentence**.

The position of the subject (*he*) and the verb (*is*) in the sentence is switched – *he is*…becomes *is he*…?)
This is one of the ways we distinguish in English between a **question** and an **affirmative sentence**.

If you are English, these are things that you have almost certainly never thought about, because they come naturally to you as a native speaker.

Consider another example in English. Compare these two sentences:

> They take sugar with their coffee.
> Do they take sugar with their coffee?

This time the word order in the **affirmative sentence** and the **question sentence** has stayed the same, but we have put the word *Do* at the beginning.

This *do* denotes that the sentence is a **question sentence**.

If the subject is *he*, *she* or *it* – the third person singular – then the word that we put at the beginning is *does*.

Why am I explaining about how to form a question in English – this is supposed to be a Spanish course, right?

Well, the reason is just to show you how wonderfully simple Spanish is on this point.

In order to change an **affirmative sentence** into a **question sentence**, you don't have to do anything at all in Spanish.

The words stay exactly the same.

Let's take the sentence *you are English*.
Hopefully, from your work in the last couple of Modules, you should know how to translate this into Spanish:

You are English.　　　　　Eres inglés.

(or Eres inglesa if the sentence refers to a girl.)

The **question sentence** is as follows:

Are you English?　　　　　¿Eres inglés?

The only difference in the written form in Spanish is that an upside down question mark appears at the beginning of the sentence.

You might think that putting an upside down question mark at the beginning of the sentence is a waste of ink, but actually it is the only way – when reading – that we can know a **question sentence** follows.

Why?

Because (unlike an English **question sentence**) the word order is exactly the same when asking a question. Nothing is added.

Isn't it easy?

No messing around with the word order or putting extra words at the beginning of the sentence as in English.

Just add a question mark!

Hang on a minute, some of you might be saying.

That's fine when something is written, but what about when it is just spoken, and there are no punctuation marks to tell you if the sentence is an affirmation or a question?

How can you tell?

The key lies in the **intonation**.

That means the sound of the sentence – the music of the words, how you say something.

When we speak, our voices are not just flat and monotonous like one of Dr Who's daleks, they go up and down.

In language, this is called the **intonation**. And it is often central to understanding the feeling or spirit in which something is said.

The only way to test your understanding of this – and your ability to distinguish between **affirmative** and **question sentences** – is to practise by listening.

The **intonation** for a **question sentence** in Spanish is the same as in English, so questions will not be difficult for you to recognize.

First of all, just look at the following list of ten sentences and try and work out what they mean.

a) Son italianos.
b) Tu hermano tiene coche.
c) Tenemos tiempo.
d) Está en la cocina.
e) Bebes cerveza.
f) Sus padres están en España.
g) Coméis carne.
h) Trabaja en la ciudad.
i) Vives con tu madre.
j) Estoy guapa.

Now listen to the eleventh track on the first CD.

TRACK 11, CD1

Let me make a quick point about question tax.

Question tax means the bit we sometimes put on the end of a **question sentence** in English.

Look at the following sentences in which I have italicized the question tax:

You are going to call him back, *aren't you?*
You were joking, *weren't you?*
I told you about that, *didn't I?*
We've brought our passports, *haven't we?*

Notice how in all these sentences the question tax is negative.

I can tell you some very good news!

To express question tax in Spanish, all you have to do is put no on the end. No suffices for all the variations in English.

So you don't have to worry about learning how to say *didn't he?* or *weren't you?* or *haven't they?* or any of the others.

Just use no.

Consider:

¿María come ajo, no?	Maria eats garlic, doesn't she?
Pero ¿la casa tiene jardín, no?	But the house has a garden, doesn't it?
¿Su padre es italiano, no?	His / Her father is Italian, isn't he?

Now it's time to learn some really important words. The following list of words are what we call **question words** and the reason should be obvious.

Cómo	How
Dónde	Where
Cuándo	When
Qué	What
Quién	Who
Por qué	Why

They are words which are often used to start a **question sentence**.

There is one important point about sentences in Spanish that use **question words**:

The verb in the sentence goes directly after the **question word**.

See how that is true in the sentences in question 1 of the Practice Activity that follows, and make sure you get the word order correct when you have to translate into Spanish in question 2.

PRACTICE ACTIVITY NINE

1. The following sentences all contain **question words**. Translate them into English:

   a) ¿Quién habla español?
   b) ¿Dónde están las patatas?
   c) ¿Cuándo trabajáis?
   d) ¿Por qué comes pescado?
   e) ¿Qué ambiciones tienes?
   f) ¿Cómo está vuestra madre?

2.   Now try and translate the following sentences from English into Spanish:

a) Why do you work in London?
b) When do your parents study Spanish?*
c) How is your friend?
d) Who drinks beer?
e) Where does he buy his shirts?
f) What do you eat in the morning?*1

   *   Don't forget that the verb follows the question word.

   *1 *in the morning* is expressed in Spanish by **por la mañana**.

Check your answers in the Answers Section.

NEGATIVE SENTENCES

Now we are going to learn how to make a **sentence negative** in Spanish.

Again, this is wonderfully simple in Spanish compared to in English.

Compare these different **negative sentences** in English:

   I don't smoke.
   She doesn't like garlic.
   They are not studying very hard.
   John isn't able to read.
   We do not want to go to the party!
   You didn't come last night.
   I won't have time to finish my homework.
   My sister hasn't seen the film.

All these **sentences** are **negative** in English.
And all of them are formed differently, depending on a number of factors.

There are many different ways to make a **negative sentence** – what a nightmare for anyone learning English!

The good news is that there's none of that in Spanish.

There is only one way to make a **negative sentence**.

To make a **sentence negative** in Spanish, all you have to do is stick the word no before the verb.

Consider:

Como carne.	I eat meat.
No como carne, soy vegetariano.	I don't eat meat, I am a vegetarian.
Soy inglés.	I am English.
No soy inglés, soy italiano.	I am not English, I am Italian.
Tengo (un) coche.*	I have a car.
No tengo (un) coche, tengo (una) moto.	I don't have a car, I have a motorbike.

* See Module 5 about article omission.

Isn't it easy?

If you want to combine a **question sentence** with a **negative sentence** (that makes what we call a negative question), the same rules apply:

| ¿No tienes tiempo? | Don't you have time? |
| ¿No eres español? | Aren't you Spanish? |

Sometimes, no is used twice in a sentence in Spanish. Consider the following situation:

Someone asks you if you are Spanish. You want to reply, *No, I am not Spanish I am English*. In English, you've got an initial negative response (*No*) and then you've got the negative sentence (*I am not*).

To say this in Spanish, you therefore need to say no twice.

¿Eres español?

No, no soy español. Soy inglés.

The first no here refers to the initial response, and the second no is the *not* in English.

Now listen to the twelfth track on the first CD.

TRACK 12, CD1

It's time now to practice for yourself the things you have studied in this Module.

1.   Translate the following sentences into English:

a) No tengo hermanos.
b) ¿Sois franceses?
c) ¿Cuándo estudian tus hijos?
d) No vivimos aquí, somos de Manchester.
e) ¿No comes carne?
f) ¿Dónde está tu hermano?
g) ¿Estás en la oficina?
h) No, no trabajo en Brighton, trabajo en Londres.
i) ¿Quién no bebe vino?
j) ¿Por qué no tienes trabajo?*

     * **trabajo**, as well as being the first person singular of the verb *to work*, is also a masculine noun meaning *job*.

2.   Translate the following into Spanish:

a) Have you got the time?*
b) Where does your mother work?*1
c) I don't drink coffee.
d) They don't study Italian, they study Spanish.
e) When does he work?
f) We don't eat meat, but we eat fish.
g) Do you speak German?
h) Why does your father write letters?*1
i) Are you (plural) in the garden?
j) Who speaks Spanish?

     *   **hora** is the word you need for *time* in this case.

     *1 Take care with the word order.

3.   In some of the above sentences, you had to combine things you had learnt in previous Modules with what you have learnt in this one, but generally I gave you sentences to translate which just tested your ability to understand and make **question** and **negative sentences**. Now it's time to try and combine everything you have learnt so far. This is called progressive revision.

Translate the following sentences into Spanish:

   a) Is your girlfriend beautiful?*
   b) Where do you buy the potatoes?
   c) I don't write books, but I write some letters.
   d) Is it a new car?
   e) Their house is very big.
   f) Do your (plural) friends drink red wine or white wine?*1
   g) When do they study Spanish?
   h) Isn't she a good teacher?
   i) Their cousins don't have a dog because they live in a flat.
   j) The bad boy doesn't live with his parents.
   k) My girlfriend isn't rich, but she is very beautiful and she eats chocolate.
   l) Who washes the car – you or your mum?*2
  m) I don't eat chicken because I am a vegetarian.
   n) Where is the market? Is it near?*3
   o) Is your father a doctor or a journalist?
   p) Do you (plural) receive presents from your uncle?
   q) My father's friends don't work in a big city.
   r) Her brother is very thin because he doesn't eat much.
   s) Why don't you sell your house? It's very small!*4
   t) Our children speak French – they have a fat teacher.

     * *your girlfriend* can either go at the beginning or at the end of the sentence.

    *1 *red wine* is **vino tinto**.

    *2 *you* is the subject pronoun – check Module 1 to remind yourself if you need to.

    *3 Whenever *where something is* is expressed in Spanish, the verb **estar** is always used (not **ser**) because we are talking about a location.

    *4 Don't forget that *small* is referring to *your house*.

Check your answers in the Answers Section.

USTED

USTED	The polite *you* (singular)
USTEDES	The polite *you* (plural)
THIRD PERSON SINGULAR	The third person singular of the verb, the one you have learnt to use for *he*, *she* or *it*.
THIRD PERSON PLURAL	The third person plural of the verb, the one you have learnt to use for *they*.

Usted in Spanish is the polite word for *you*.

In English, when we are talking to another person we call them *you*.
The word *you* is used for everybody, it doesn't matter if I am addressing the Queen or a stray cat – I use the word *you* for both of them.

In Spanish, this is not the case.

You have already learnt the words tú for *you* (singular) and vosotros for *you* (plural) back in Module 1.

But the word usted also means *you*, as does ustedes, which is the plural version.

Usted and ustedes have to be used when we want to show courtesy or respect.

I didn't introduce these polite words for *you* in the first Module when we studied the present tense (the Present Simple) because it would have been one thing too many to learn at that time.

It was important at first to lay the basic rules about how the verbs work (i.e. different endings denoting which person is doing the action of the verb). That concept should now be very familiar to you.

Let's now have a look at how usted works.

The part of the verb that is used for the formal *you* (usted) is not the same as the part of the verb used for tú, the informal word.

Tú, as you know, is the second person singular.
But usted is used with the **third person singular**, the same ending that is used for *he*, *she* and *it*.

And the part used for the plural formal *you* (ustedes) is the **third person plural** – the same that is used for *they*.

Let's look again at one of our model verbs from Module 1, Mirar. Alongside you can see the subject pronouns that correspond to the different parts of the verb.

miro	yo
miras	tú
mira	él, ella, **usted**
miramos	nosotros
miráis	vosotros
miran	ellos / ellas / **ustedes**

I hope you have noticed that there are two additions here from what you learnt in Module 1.

The additions are usted and ustedes.

They are also subject pronouns.

So, mira - the **third person singular** of mirar - can actually mean four different things:

He looks at
She looks at
It looks at
+
You (polite) look at

And miran – the **third person plural** of mirar – can mean two different things:

They look at
+
You (polite plural) look at

Usted always takes the **third person singular** part of the verb, and ustedes always takes the **third person plural** part of the verb.

Let's see how it works in practice.

Let's imagine that someone is coming to your house for dinner. You are going to use usted with them, not tú. You are about to dress the salad and want to know if your guest eats garlic or not. If he doesn't, you won't add the garlic to the dressing you have prepared.

You are going to ask him / her, *Do you eat garlic?*

If you were asking someone informally, you would say:

¿Comes ajo?

This is the way that you have learnt to say *you eat* (or *do you eat...?*, as in this case).

What you are learning in this Module is that there is another way to say this, a formal or polite way.

So in our imaginary situation here, you have to use the **third person singular** of the verb comer and say:

¿Come ajo?

This also means *do you eat garlic?*
The difference is that it is the polite form.

Later in the Module we will talk about when you should use the polite form and when you should use the informal form.

Now, an obvious question arises.

This sentence – ¿Come ajo? – has more than one possible meaning.
It could mean any one of the following three things:

Does he eat garlic?
Does she eat garlic?
Do you (polite) eat garlic?

Of course, the speaker is fully aware of what he / she is intending to say. But there are occasions when it might not be obvious to the hearers who the verb is referring to.

You have come across this concept of potential confusion before, in Module 4.

The truth is that in most cases, it is clear from the context who the verb refers to.

To remove any potential confusion, however, we can use the subject pronouns.

Consider the following two sentences which are identical in meaning:

> ¿Usted come ajo?
> ¿Come usted ajo?

By putting usted either before or after the verb, all doubt has been removed as to who the verb is referring to.
Now it is completely clear that the sentence means *do you eat garlic?* as opposed to *does he / she eat garlic?*

Equally, if I said, ¿Él come ajo? it becomes completely clear that I am asking if he eats garlic, because I am using the subject pronoun él – the word that means *he*.

Sometimes the subject pronouns are used anyway – even when there is no potential confusion – just for emphasis.

This is something difficult to explain and give examples of, because there are no 'rules' about when to use the subject pronouns.
Spanish people themselves couldn't explain when to use them – they just do, naturally.

If you spend long enough listening to native Spanish speakers, you will be able to 'feel' the sense of when to use them.
Getting a natural feel for a language is a very important thing, but it only really comes after living in a place where that language is spoken for a considerable amount of time.

In our example situation here, even if there was only you and your guest in the room, it would be perfectly acceptable to use the subject pronoun usted and say:

> ¿Usted come ajo?

Now imagine you wanted to ask your guest if he / she spoke English.
This is what you would need to say:

¿(**Usted**) habla inglés?
¿Habla (**usted**) inglés?

Notice the two places in the sentence where you can put the usted. Both are totally correct and there is no difference between them.

Look at the following questions that might be asked during the course of the evening in our imaginary situation:

¿Bebe vino?
¿Es español?

In the following two questions, a question word is used.
Whenever a question word is used, the subject pronoun can't be put before the verb.
It must go after the verb (or occasionally at the very beginning of the sentence).

¿Dónde vive (**usted**)?
¿Cuándo trabaja (**usted**)?

This applies to all subject pronouns. But bear in mind that usually they are not used at all.

I hope you had no trouble in understanding what the questions meant.

Ustedes works in exactly the same way.

If you are addressing more than one person in a formal way, you have to use the **third person plural**, the same part of the verb that is used for *they*.

¿Beben vino?
¿Son españoles?
¿Dónde viven?
¿Cuándo trabajan?

These sentences are the plural versions of the ones above.

Now, here's something important to bear in mind.

Do you remember the possessive adjectives? We studied them in Module 4.

They are the words which tell us who something belongs to. For example:

my trousers
your sweets
his desk

our friends
your letters
their house

The words in italics are all examples of possesive adjectives – I am sure you remember something about them. Have a look back at Module 4 now if you want to refresh your memory.

In relation to usted and ustedes, the point is this.

You have learnt that to say *your house*, for example, you need to say tu casa. Or, if you were talking to more than one person, you would need to say vuestra casa.

But in both cases, that is the informal way.

If you are addressing someone as usted or some people as ustedes, you would need to use the **third person singular / plural** possessive adjective. Like this:

Su casa es muy bonita.   Your house is very beautiful.

Su and Sus are the possessive adjectives that you have learnt are used for *his*, *her*, *its* and *their*.

What you are learning here is that they are also used for the polite *your* – when you are addressing someone as usted or ustedes.

Just as usted takes the **third person singular** part of the verb (the same part that is used for *he*, *she* and *it*), so usted takes the **third person singular** form of the possessive adjectives (the same that is used for *his*, *her* and *its*).

And with ustedes it is the same – the **third person plural** form of the possessive adjectives (which is the same as the singular form anyway – su and sus) is used.

Look at these example sentences which demonstrate this:

¿Cómo está su mujer?   How is your wife?
Sus perros son muy grandes.   Your dogs are very big.
¿Dónde está su hijo?   Where is your son?
No tengo su dirección.   I haven't got your address.

This can all seem a bit confusing at first.

The problem is the multiple meanings of su and sus.

Su casa can actually mean a staggering six different things:

his house, her house, its house, your (polite singular) *house, their house, your* (polite plural) *house.*

Usually, you can know from the context who *su* is referring to.

If it isn't clear who *su* refers to, then you can clarify it like this, using "*de* + subject pronoun".

La casa de él	his house
La casa de ella	her house
La casa de **usted**	your house
La casa de ellos	their house
La casa de **ustedes**	your (plural) house

So, the big question to consider now is:

When is it necessary to use *usted* and *ustedes*, the polite forms for *you*, instead of *tú* and *vosotros*, which are the informal forms and the ones you originally learnt?

There are not hard and fast rules about this, only guidelines which are really based on common sense.

Firstly, in business or formal situations, you should use *usted*.

Expect people to use *usted* with you when you are in a restaurant or bank or any situation where you are receiving a public service, and use it back to the other person.

Use *usted* when you are introduced to someone about ten or more years older than you. It would be considered cheeky not to do so.

There was a time in Spain when children always used *usted* and *ustedes* with their parents, but that is not often the case now. *Usted* is certainly less common than it used to be, but you must not bypass it and imagine that you don't need it. If you want to speak Spanish properly, you need to know how and when to use *usted* correctly.

If you are in doubt in a situation whether or not to use *usted*, err on the side of caution by using it. Nobody can be seriously offended if you use *usted* when *tú* would suffice, but you can offend by not using *usted* when you should.

If you use *usted* with someone, they might tell you that it's not necessary and that you can use *tú* with them. From that time onward you never need use *usted* with them again.

There is an interesting verb in Spanish – tutear. It means "to use tú".

Consider this example:

There are two men who have just met each other having a conversation. One of them is a few years older than the other one. The younger one asks the other:

¿Trabaja (**usted**) en Barcelona?

Notice how he is using the **third person singular** of the verb. If he wanted to be informal, he would say:

¿Trabajas en Barcelona?

But he has used the first sentence – he is being polite.
The older man doesn't want the younger man to use usted with him, so he replies:

Tutéame, hombre!

Don't worry about the grammar of this sentence (we haven't studied it yet), but it could be translated in the following way:

"Use tú with me, my friend!"

In other words, he is giving the younger man permission to address him informally.

Listen out for that one – someone may say it to you!

If you use usted with someone the first time you meet them, and they don't tell you to use tú, then continue with usted always.

Now listen to the thirteenth track on the first CD.

TRACK 13, CD1

1. In each of the following sentences the subject is either **usted** or **ustedes**. Translate them into English:

    a) ¿Son italianos?
    b) ¿Tiene dos hermanas o tres?
    c) ¿Escribe cartas por la mañana?
    d) ¿Bebe café o té?
    e) ¿Compran pescado en el mercado?*
    f) ¿Vive en un piso?
    g) ¿Dónde están ahora?
    h) ¿No fuman?
    i) ¿Estudia mucho o poco?
    j) ¿Hablan español bien?

    * **en** in this sentence would be translated as *at*.

2. Translate the following sentences into Spanish, using the formal *you*:

    a) You (plural) don't drink tea.*
    b) Do you (singular) have my dictionary?
    c) When do you (plural) eat dinner?*[1]
    d) Why do you (singular) have three cars?
    e) You (plural) have three houses, don't you?
    f) When do you (singular) speak French?
    g) What do you (plural) buy in the supermarket?
    h) Your (singular) friend is very thin.*[2]
    i) Your (plural) friends don't work in England, do they?
    j) Do you (singular) study Spanish now?

    * Remember that the position of "**no**" is before the verb.

    *[1] In Spanish you have to use the article with the names of the meals. So here you would say "the dinner".

    *[2] This sentence would actually be identical if it was plural.

Check your answers in the Answers Section.

It's time now for another Progress Check. Like before, this is going to involve combining everything you have learnt in the first eight Modules. The point of this is for you to see how well you are assimilating what you are learning. Take your time before starting these exercises. I really want to encourage you to think about the best way for you to use this Progress Check. Before the last one, I told you to use it to your advantage and do the exercises in the way that would best help you, whether that meant revising first everything you have studied so far and then attempting them, or trying them without any revision to see how much you remember.

It's only a suggestion, but this time you could try the other way to the one you used last time. That way you could compare and perhaps decide which way is more beneficial for you. However you decide to approach these exercises, do remember how important they are, and that how well you do will reflect exactly your progress. There will be two more Progress Checks in the course - one after Module 12 and another one at the end (after Module 16).

If you don't do as well as you hoped, please don't despair! Fight any feelings of discouragement that you may have. You've always got the course to refer back to, and if you persevere, I am sure that in time you will be able to eradicate whatever mistakes you might have.

PART ONE

Translate the following sentences into Spanish:

1   I don't speak French, but my girlfriend is French.

2.   Do you (polite plural) drink tea, coffee or juice in the morning?* & *1

3.   Their parents use my computer.

4.   His children don't work in the city.

5.   Do you (polite) work in an office?

6.   Do you (plural) eat French food?*2

7. We don't have any money.*3

8. They drink milk in the morning and wine at night.*4

9. Do your (polite) students use computers, or only books?*5

10. My brother listens to the radio when he writes letters.

* Do you remember how to say *in the morning*?

*1 *or* in Spanish is just "**o**".

*2 You have to use the article *the*.

*3 You don't need to translate the word *any*.

*4 Do you remember how to say *at night*?

*5 The word for *only* is **solamente**.

PART TWO

There is one mistake in each of the following ten sentences. Find the mistake, correct it, and then write a translation of the corrected sentence. See the example.

e.g. Mi hermano <u>bebo</u> el té.
Mi hermano bebe el té.   My brother drinks the tea.

1. La gorda niña no come mucho.

2. ¿Tienes usted hora?

3. Trabajo no mucho en la oficina.

4. Tu novia es en la cocina.

5. Carlos, ¿tu esposa es inglés?

6. Nuestras padres no viven en la ciudad.

7. Comemos unos patatas.

8. Mi hermana es una profesora.

9. Roberto's primos están enfadados.

10. No bebe café en la mañana.

PART THREE

In this exercise, translate the following sentences into English. On occasions you will need to be flexible with your translation. In other words, don't translate literally if the literal translation in English doesn't sound natural or correct. Instead, work out what the meaning is and then express it in a natural way in English.

1. No tenemos una casa confortable, pero el jardín es muy grande.

2. Los padres de mi amigo Juan no compran pescado en el supermercado.

3. Las maletas son pequeñas pero pesan bastante.

4. En la opinión de mi profesor, los exámenes de matemáticas no son difíciles.

5. Nuestro dinero está en una caja debajo de nuestra cama.

6. Estoy triste porque mi hermano no está casado.

7. La mayoría de los estudiantes famosos en mi colegio no beben cerveza.

8. Nuestro nuevo abogado es delgado y un poco loco, pero no vive en la ciudad.

9. Tengo una pregunta - ¿necesitamos cebollas?

10. ¿Dónde está el chico rico con su café italiano?

PART FOUR

Each of the following sentences contains *you*. For each sentence, write out all the possible translations in Spanish – the formal ones (using **usted** and **ustedes**), and the informal ones (using **tú** and **vosotros**). See the example.

e.g.   Do you speak Spanish?

¿Hablas español?	(Informal)
¿Habla español?	(Polite)
¿Habláis español?	(Informal plural)
¿Hablan español?	(Polite plural)

1. Where do you study English?

2. When do you work?

3. What do you eat at night?

4. Do you listen to the radio in the morning?*

5. Do you live in a house or a flat?

6. Do you write letters or e-mails?

7. Do you sell tobacco?

8. Do you answer in Spanish?

9. Why do you have a computer in your garage?*1

10. Is your teacher Italian?*2

* Take care in this sentence with the gender of the Spanish word for *radio* – it's one of the few exceptions to the rules you have learnt about noun genders. (See Module 3)

*1 Don't forget to change the possessive adjectives as well as the verb.

*2 Here you only need to change the form of the possessive adjective, which means that there are only three different possible answers. See if you can work out why.

COMMON EXPRESSIONS

This Module will be slightly different in the sense that it deals with some practical speaking.

So far in the course, you have studied a lot about how the Spanish language works.

If you do pursue your studies of Spanish beyond this course, you will see the immense value of the foundation that you are building here.

But what most people get excited about when they study a language is the thought of being able to say things to native speakers and being understood.

In this Module, you will have a bit of a breather from the theory of Spanish and work on some basic communication skills.

You will learn how to introduce yourself, greet people, and say some very common expressions.

It's very important to realize – and you will have been doing so throughout this course – that often it is not possible to translate directly from English into Spanish.

Often the way to convey the meaning of something is different in another language, and it doesn't make sense if we translate directly or literally.

A good example of this is the first common expression I have listed underneath. Here it is:

Hola, me llamo…   Hello, my name is…

If I translate the Spanish expression exactly (i.e. literally) then it means "Hello, I call myself…."

But that doesn't make sense in English.

Although the meaning is the same, we say it in a different way. We say:

Hello, my name is…

If you were an interpreter, interpreting from Spanish to English for someone, you wouldn't interpret this sentence literally.

You wouldn't say about the person you were interpreting for:

"He calls himself Mark."

You would of course say:

"His name is Mark."

Translating and interpreting is about conveying the meaning that is intended in the most natural way possible in the other language.

It would be easicr if all languages expressed ideas in exactly the same way, but they don't.
In this expression, me llamo is actually part of a special kind of verb called a reflexive verb.
The next Module deals with reflexive verbs, so don't worry about them just yet!

I hope this example demonstrates what I mean when I say that often we can't translate literally.

So, we have to learn 'the Spanish way' to say what we want to say.

From the expressions that you are about to learn in this Module, it is inevitable that new grammar points will arise. You will probably find you have some questions. (i.e. Why do they say it like that?)

Be patient with your questions for the moment.

What I want to get you doing here is practice speaking in Spanish.

Some of the grammar points that come up will be covered in later Modules of the course, and I have indicated where that is the case.

Other points will not be covered, as they involve things that are too far advanced to get into yet.

The point of this particular Module is not to explain more grammar, but to get you speaking in Spanish.

For that reason, the CD will play a big part in this Module.

As well as having questions about things you don't understand, I also hope that you will be able to see how we are applying a lot of the things we have learnt in the course so far.

If you have ever looked at a Spanish phrase book or spent time in a Spanish speaking country, then some of the expressions here may well be familiar to you.

Remember though, it is impossible to practice too much.
If this does seem rather easy to you, bear in mind that the CD activities will help to cement your knowledge.
And if this is all or mostly new to you, you can practice the activities in the privacy of your own home – without disruptions – as much as you want to.

I haven't put a translation alongside any of the expressions that you should already understand from what we have studied in the course so far, or where you should be able to guess the meaning through common sense.

Brief notes follow each expression where necessary.

With very common expressions, it is better at first to just learn them as they are, even if you don't understand why you have to say them in the way that you do.

Hola, me llamo…   **Hello, my name is**…

This me llamo is part of the reflexive verb llamarse – this is dealt with in the next Module.

¿Cómo te llamas?   **What is your name?**
¿Cómo se llama usted?   **What is your name?**

Cómo actually means *how*, so the question literally translated means, "How do you call yourself?" which makes no sense in English, although you can see what they are driving at!

Soy inglés / inglesa / español / española.

Remember you need to put an "a" on the end instead of an "o" if you are female. Notice also that it is not necessary to start an adjective of nationality with a capital letter.

Somos ingleses / españoles.

This sentence could be used if you were introducing you and your partner, or your family.

Soy de Inglaterra / España.   **I am from England / Spain.**
Somos de Inglaterra / España.   **We are from England / Spain.**

Notice how the names of countries in Spanish do need a capital letter.

Encantado / a	**Pleased / Nice to meet you**
Mucho gusto	**Pleased / Nice to meet you**

Don't forget to change encantado to encantada if you are female.

Vivo / Vivimos en Inglaterra / España.

Estoy / Estamos de vacaciones.   **I / We are on holiday.**

Estar de vacaciones means *to be on holiday*, so all you have to do is use the appropiate part of the verb (estoy, estás, está etc) and the de vacaciones bit stays the same.

Buenos días	**Good morning**
Buenas tardes	**Good afternoon / evening**
Buenas noches	**Good night**

Notice how in Spanish these expressions are always plural.

Notice also how buenos changes to buenas in the latter two – this is because tarde and noche are both feminine nouns.

Día on the other hand – and rather surprisingly given that it ends in an "a" – is a masculine noun. It is one of the exceptions (see Module 14) to the rule that you learnt in Module 3.

Buenas noches, like in English, is used only as the last thing you say to someone in a day – in other words, when you are leaving someone's house or when you are off to bed.

¿Hace buen tiempo hoy, no?	**It's lovely today, isn't it?**
Hace mal tiempo.	**It's not nice weather.**
Hace calor.	**It's hot.**
Hace frío.	**It's cold.**
Hace sol.	**It's sunny.**

For many weather expressions in Spanish, they don't use the verb *to be* like we do in English.

They use the verb hacer, which means *to do* or *to make*.
Module 15 deals with weather expressions.

¿Cómo estás?	
¿Cómo está usted?	
¿Usted, cómo está?	
¿Y tú?	**And you?**
¿Qué tal?	**How are you doing?**
¿Cómo te va?	**How are things going?**

The translation of these last two is flexible – they are very common expressions and amount to just variations on asking someone how they are.

Estoy (muy) bien, gracias.	**I am (very) well, thanks.**
Estoy mal / mala.	**I am not well.**
Estoy regular.	**I am so-so.**

These are the typical responses to the above questions.

¿Qué haces / hace?	**What do you do?**
¿En qué trabajas / trabaja?	**What line of work are you in?**

In both these cases the alternative given is for usted. I hope you realized that!

Soy médico / profesor / abogado.	**I am a doctor / teacher / lawyer.**

9

Don't forget you have to leave out the article in Spanish when you say what someone does.

Adios, hasta luego	**Goodbye, see you later**
Nos veremos	**See you soon**
(Muchas) gracias	**Thank you (very much)**
De nada	**Not at all**
Lo siento (mucho)	**I am (very) sorry**

Now listen to the fourteenth track on the first CD.

TRACK 14, CD1

Now it's time to imagine a potentially real situation. Imagine you have just met a native Spanish speaker who knows nothing about you. Using some of the expressions that you have been considering here in Module 9, prepare a simple introduction of yourself. It need not be long, but it should include at least three different facts about you. After you have prepared it, practise reading it out loud.

Now listen to the fifteenth track on the first CD.

TRACK 15, CD1

Now listen to the sixteenth and final track on the first CD.

TRACK 16, CD1

BOOT VERBS AND REFLEXIVE VERBS

BOOT VERBS	Verbs that change their formation in the stem.
RADICALLY-CHANGING VERBS	Another term for boot verbs
REFLEXIVE VERBS	Verbs that put "se" on the end and turn the meaning of the verb onto oneself.
REFLEXIVE PRONOUNS	me, te, se, nos, os, se

BOOT VERBS

Boot verbs were mentioned back in Module 5, when we considered the verb tener. They are also called **radically-changing verbs**.

Radical comes from the Latin word for root, and root you may remember is another word for stem.
So, **radically-changing verbs** are verbs which change in the stem.

That means that when a verb is conjugated in the present tense, the stem changes from the stem of the infinitive.

Let's demonstrate this.

You will remember from Module 1 that when we conjugate a regular verb in the present tense, we separate the stem from the ending, like this:

HABL-AR

To form the different parts then, we keep the same stem and add different endings. This should be old hat for you by now.

However, with **boot verbs**, the stem changes in certain parts of the verb.

So, the first thing to realize is that **boot verbs** are - by nature - irregular verbs.

A regular verb keeps the same stem. By definition, **boot verbs** are verbs that change the stem.

There are three different stem changes that can occur:

1. Some verbs with "e" in the infinitive change to "ie".
2. Some verbs with "o" in the infinitive change to "ue" (occasionally "u" to "ue"*).
3. Some verbs with "e" in the infinitive change to "i".

   * Jugar (*to play*) is an example of this.

Tener - which you studied in Module 5 - was an example of the first kind. The "e" in the stem changes to an "ie" in certain parts of the verb.

Tengo	Tenemos
Tienes	Tenéis
Tiene	Tienen

Just as in Module 5, I have shaded the three parts of the verb (the second and third persons singular and the third person plural) to show the boot shape.

Boot verbs can be in any of the three categories - AR, ER or IR.

There are other **boot verbs** in which the stem changes in the first person singular as well.

The verb Pensar (*to think*) is an example of this.

Pienso	Pensamos
Piensas	Pensáis
Piensa	Piensan

Here the change occurs in the whole of the singular and the third person plural. So the boot shape is bigger!

So, one way to remember this is to think in terms of two kinds of **boot verbs** – ankle-high **boot verbs** and knee-high **boot verbs**.

Tener is an example of an ankle-high **boot verb**, as the stem change does not occur in the first person singular. The boot shape is therefore smaller.

Pensar, on the other hand, is an example of a knee-high **boot verb**, as the change occurs in the whole of the singular and the third person plural. The boot shape is therefore bigger.

All **boot verbs**, whether ankle-high or knee-high, revert back in the first and second person plural to using the same stem as in the infinitive.

Let's look at some examples of the different kinds of **boot verbs**.

1.   Verbs that change from "e" to "ie"

Cerrar	to close
Empezar	to begin
Venir*	to come

2.   Verbs that change from "o" to "ue"

Poder	to be able
Morir	to die
Volver	to return

3.   Verbs that change from "e" to "i"

Pedir	to ask for
Seguir	to follow / continue
Decir*	to say / tell

* Venir and Decir both have other **irregular** features apart from being **boot verbs**. You will see this in a moment in the Practice Activity.

So far, you have only seen written out examples of the first kind of **boot verbs** – tener and pensar.

Have a look now at one example of each of the other two kinds:

PODER (o to ue)

Puedo	Podemos
Puedes	Podéis
Puede	Pueden

PEDIR (e to i)

Pido	Pedimos
Pides	Pedís
Pide	Piden

I hope you can see that both these verbs are knee-high **boot verbs**.

PRACTICE ACTIVITY TWELVE

1.   Have a go now at writing out the following **radically-changing verbs** (all
     of which appear above) in the Present Tense. They are all knee-high **boot
     verbs** (i.e. all of them have a stem change in the first person singular).
     Write them out in the order in which they appear below.

     a) Seguir
     b) Cerrar
     c) Morir
     d) Volver
     e) Empezar

2.   Now do the same with "Venir" and "Decir". Underneath I have given you
     the first person singular (which is an added irregular feature of these two
     verbs). Just follow the pattern you have studied in this Module. You will
     see from the first persons singular underneath that "venir" is an ankle-high
     boot verb (because the stem in the first person singular is unchanged)
     whereas "decir" is a knee-high **boot verb**.

     a) Vengo etc, etc
     b) Digo etc, etc

3.   Now write out the following **boot verbs** which you haven't seen before and find out what they mean. They are all knee-high **boot verbs**.

   a) Encontrar (o-ue)
   b) Dormir (o-ue)
   c) Querer (e-ie)
   d) Sentir (e-ie)
   e) Entender (e-ie)
   f) Preferir (e-ie)

Check your answers in the Answers Section.

How can you know if a verb is a **boot verb** or not?

The answer is you can't.

Boot verbs just have to be remembered, like all irregular verbs.

Any half decent dictionary will indicate **boot verbs**, probably by putting the letters "ie", "ue" or "i" in brackets after the infinitive.

Also, most decent size dictionaries have a verb section either in the middle or at the end where you can check other irregular features of some **boot verbs** (like tener, venir and decir).

The good thing is that in this Module you have not only been introduced to them, but have pretty much learnt all there is to know about them and have looked at the most common ones.

In a moment we are going to move on to the second part of this Module and talk about another kind of verb, but before we do, listen to the first track on the second CD.

TRACK 1, CD2

REFLEXIVE VERBS

This might be a good time to break if you feel like your brain has taken in enough for one day.
We all take time to absorb something new. Even if you feel you have understood something perfectly, there is still a process of assimilation that has to take place.

Treating this Module as two separate Modules would be my advice, but that's up to you.

Reflexive verbs are extremely common in Spanish, but what are they?

Basically, how they differ from a normal verb is that they turn the action of the verb onto oneself.

Let me start by giving you two examples in English to help explain.

To wash is a normal verb, but *to wash oneself* is a **reflexive verb**.
Similarly, *to cut* is a normal verb, but *to cut oneself* is a **reflexive verb**.

Those two examples you will see in Spanish in a moment, along with other **reflexive verbs**.

However, there are **verbs** which are **reflexive** in Spanish but which are not translated in English as *to do something oneself*.

For example, the **verbs** *to get up* and *to go to bed* are both **reflexive** in Spanish.

So **reflexive verbs** - like **boot verbs** - just have to be learnt.

You have to learn and remember which **verbs** are **reflexive** and which are just normal.

The reason you have to know and remember which **verbs** are **reflexive** and which are not is because **reflexive verbs** are formed differently.

Let's look now at the formation of **reflexive verbs**.
We'll start with one of the examples I have given - *to cut / to cut oneself*.

To cut is a regular AR verb - the verb cortar.
To cut oneself is a **reflexive verb** - cortarse.

Reflexive verbs add se to the infinitive.

When it comes to conjugating the verb, there is a **reflexive pronoun** for each person of the verb that has to be put in front of the part of the verb.

Have a look below at the conjugation of first, cortar, and then cortarse:

Corto	I cut
Cortas	You cut
Corta	He / She / It cuts
Cortamos	We cut
Cortáis	You cut
Cortan	They cut

Me corto	I cut myself
Te cortas	You cut yourself
Se corta	He / She cuts himself / herself
Nos cortamos	We cut ourselves
Os cortáis	You cut yourselves
Se cortan	They cut themselves

So:

Corto las patatas means *I cut the potatoes.*
Me corto means *I cut myself.*

So if a **verb** is **reflexive**, it is always formed using these **reflexive pronouns**.

Reflexive verbs can come from any of the three types of verb – AR, ER or IR. They can also be irregular verbs, and many **reflexive verbs** are in fact **boot verbs**. You will see some examples shortly.

You have just seen the verb cortarse. In the last Module you learnt how to say what your name is in Spanish. A **reflexive verb** is used to say this, the verb llamarse.

Llamo means *I call*, but me llamo means literally "I call myself".

This was explained in the last Module. Have a look back if you need to refresh your memory.

10

PRACTICE ACTIVITY THIRTEEN

Now it's time to practice writing out some **reflexive verbs**. If this seems like a daunting task, let me suggest you start by doing it in two steps. Write the verb out normally first, and then add in the **reflexive pronouns (me, te, se, nos, os, se)** afterwards. Don't forget that they go before the parts of the verb.

1.   Write out the following regular **reflexive verbs**:

   a) llamarse
   b) levantarse
   c) preocuparse
   d) prepararse
   e) lavarse
   f) aburrirse*

   * Notice that "aburrirse" is an IR verb.

2. The following verbs are knee-high **boot verbs** as well as being **reflexive**. Again, if this gives you a headache, just do it in stages. Do the **boot verb** bit first, and afterwards put the **reflexive pronouns** in. At this stage, it's better to do it slowly and correctly, and doing it in stages will give you more chance to get it right. Don't bite off more than you can chew. Make it easy for yourself for the moment. The important thing right now is just to get you applying what you have learnt by doing these exercises.

Write out the following **reflexive** knee-high **boot verbs**:

a) sentirse (e-ie)
b) sentarse (e-ie)
c) acostarse (o-ue)
d) despedirse (e-i)
e) divertirse (e-ie)
f) perderse (e-ie)

Check your answers in the Answers Section.

Here are a couple of further points about **reflexive verbs**:

1. To make a reflexive verb negative, you do the same as you would for any other verb. You have to put the word no before the verb – with reflexive verbs that means putting it before the reflexive pronoun, as reflexive pronouns are part of the verb. For example:

No **me** levanto temprano.
I don't get up early.

No **se** llama Federico, se llama Fernando.
His name isn't Frederick, it's Fernando.

2. Many **verbs** can be both **reflexive** and normal. You have already seen this with the verb llamar / llamarse. Often a **verb** can be made **reflexive** to give this "oneself" meaning. For example:

Me hablo cuando estoy solo.
I speak / talk to myself when I am alone.

Se mira en el espejo.
He looks at himself in the mirror.

Now listen to the second track on the second CD.

TRACK 2, CD2

This Module has contained a lot, and there's probably a good chance that you could be confused by some points. Never worry if you feel you don't understand something properly. You can go over the material as often as you need and repeat the exercises as many times as you want to. Give yourself time and things will more than likely become clear. The audio material will also help to clarify and cement what you have learned here. Listen to it as many times as you need. That is what it is there for.

Although you have already had practice in writing out **boot verbs** and **reflexive verbs**, you haven't had any opportunity to put them into sentences. Because this Module has contained a lot of information, there is another Practice Activity here to help you to further cement what you have studied.

PRACTICE ACTIVITY FOURTEEN

1. Translate the following sentences into English:

    a) Sus padres vuelven a casa por la tarde.
    b) Se aburre cuando está solo.
    c) Nos levantamos muy temprano.
    d) Mi hijo no quiere dormir cuando bebe coca-cola.
    e) ¿Os sentís tristes?
    f) No puedo encontrar las llaves de la casa.*
    g) Ella se lava por la mañana.*1
    h) Tiene dos nietos – se llaman Antonio y María.
    i) La gente muere, es una realidad.
    j) ¿Quieres jugar en el parque?

    *   **puedo** is from the verb *to be able*, which is nearly always translated as *can* in English.

    *1 Notice that the subject pronoun (**ella**) is used here to clarify who **se lava** refers to.

2. Translate the following sentences into Spanish:

a) Her father's name is Juan.
b) We can't study today, I haven't got my books.*
c) You (plural) enjoy yourself a lot in the park, don't you?
d) Do you go to bed late?
e) Their children don't tell lies.*1
f) I get lost when I don't have a map.
g) I don't eat much fish, I prefer meat.
h) Do you (plural) get bored in the lesson?
i) Our son is fat, and we worry.
j) They follow the teacher's instructions.

   *   *can't* is from the verb *to be able*.

  *1 *to tell lies* is **decir mentiras**.

Check your answers in the Answers Section.

DEMONSTRATIVE ADJECTIVES

DEMONSTRATIVE ADJECTIVES   The words that mean *this*, *that*, *these*, *those* (este, esta, estos, estas, esto, ese, esa, esos, esto, eso).

Demonstrative adjectives are very important.

With the exception of esto and eso, they are always followed by a noun (e.g. *this* table, *that* mountain, *these* houses, *those* students.)

They are called **demonstrative adjectives** because they demonstrate which "thing" I am talking about (e.g. *this* man as opposed to *that* man).

What you studied in Module 3 is very helpful in connection with what you are going to study here.

You will remember how we have to use different articles (the words meaning *the* or *a* or *some*) depending on whether the noun is masculine singular, masculine plural, feminine singular or feminine plural. Have a look back to remind yourself if you need to.

It is the same with the **demonstrative adjectives**.

Let's take each one individually.

THIS

In English we can say *this* man or *this* woman – we use the same word for *this*.

But in Spanish, that is not the case.

There are actually three words for *this* in Spanish, and three words for *that*. For now, however, we are going to look at just two of them.

One of them is for masculine singular nouns.
The other one is for feminine singular nouns.

The third word that means *this* will be dealt with later in the Module.

Este is used for masculine singular nouns.

este hombre	this man
este libro	this book
este curso	this course

Esta is used for feminine singular nouns.

esta casa	this house
esta información	this information
esta botella de vino	this bottle of wine*

> * Here the noun is *bottle*, and hence the feminine form of the **demonstrative adjective** is used. If I were to say *this wine* I would have to use the masculine form and say este vino, because wine in Spanish is masculine.

One thing that you may be thinking is that the feminine form for *this* is the same word as the third person singular form of the verb estar.

Actually, the third person singular form of estar (está, meaning *he is / she is / it is*) has an accent, whereas the **demonstrative adjective** esta has no accent on it.

The use of accents changes the stress on a word and therefore the pronunciation, but it is impossible to demonstrate this without audio material.

You will be learning about that in Module 14, so for now just bear in mind the fact that an accent differentiates between the part of the verb estar and the **demonstrative adjective**.

está	he / she / it is
esta	this

THESE

In English, the plural word for *this* is *these*.

And just as in the singular, there are two words in Spanish for *these*, depending on whether the plural noun is masculine or feminine.

You should be getting used to this by now!

Estos is used for masculine plural nouns.

estos coches	these cars
estos periódicos	these newspapers
estos pantalones	these trousers

Estas is used for feminine plural nouns.

estas chicas	these girls
estas revistas	these magazines
estas playas	these beaches

This feminine plural form looks like the second person singular of estar. But again, as with esta the singular form, an accent distinguishes between them:

| estás | you are |
| estas | these |

THAT

When it comes to the word for *that* the same principle applies.
There are two words for *that* (plus a third one which you will learn about shortly), depending on whether the noun is masculine or feminine.

Ese is used for masculine nouns.

ese plátano	that banana
ese pueblo	that town
ese sombrero	that hat

Esa is used for feminine nouns.

esa mujer	that woman
esa casa	that house
esa ciudad	that city

Notice how the only difference between *this* and *that* in Spanish is the removal of the letter "t" (este becomes ese, and esta becomes esa).

THOSE

And when it comes to *those*, the same principle applies again.
There are two words, depending on whether the noun is masculine or feminine.

Esos is used for masculine plural nouns.

esos planes	those plans
esos discos	those records
esos paises	those countries

Esas is used for feminine plural nouns.

esas cosas	those things
esas flores	those flowers
esas cervezas	those beers

This is fairly easy theory, but it's difficult to get used to in practice.

The concept of some kinds of words (articles, adjectives and now **demonstrative adjectives**) having different forms (masculine, feminine, singular, plural) is one that you are probably getting used to by now.

But in practice – especially when it comes to speaking – it is difficult to remember at the time of making a sentence.

Of course, if you make a mistake and say something like este chica instead of esta chica, Spanish people are going to understand you.

But it will sound clumsy to their ears.

There's a further point to be made here.

Earlier on in the Module I said there were actually three words that meant *this* and three words that meant *that*.

You have learnt the masculine and feminine singular forms. Just to remind you, they are:

este / esta	this
ese / esa	that

These forms always go together with a noun.

However, sometimes we say *this* or *that* without a noun. For example, we can say:

"This is crazy!"
"That is the problem."

In these two examples the **demonstrative adjective** is not connected to any noun. *This is crazy!* simply refers to the situation.

Similarly in the second sentence, *that* is referring to something, but not one particular noun. It's referring to a fact, for example, *the fact that the workers want a pay rise, that is the problem*.

So there are other words for *this* and *that* when they are not spoken or written in association with a particular noun, like in these two example situations.

The words are:

Esto   this
Eso   that

So the translation of the two sentences above would be:

Esto es loco!
Eso es el problema.

In these two sentences, the **demonstrative adjectives** are not connected to any noun. They are followed by the verb *to be*. You will see more examples of this in the Practice Activity to come.

Now listen to the third track on the second CD.

11

TRACK 3, CD2

PRACTICE ACTIVITY FIFTEEN

1.   Translate the following sentences from Spanish into English:

  a) Puedes dormir en esta habitación.
  b) Compro estos caramelos cada semana en el mercado.
  c) Esa es la niña que come mucho chocolate.*
  d) Esas revistas están en la mesa en la cocina.
  e) Estas naranjas son muy buenas – son de Sevilla.
  f) Lo siento, pero eso no es lógico.

g) Queremos comprar este piso porque tiene balcón.

h) Ese paquete es un regalo de Navidad.

i) Esos niños siempre juegan al fútbol en la calle.*1

j) Esto es maravilloso!

> * As I am sure you have realized, **que** in this sentence has to be translated as *who*.

> *1 The verb **jugar** is followed by "**a**".

2. Translate the following sentences from English into Spanish:

a) Those boys are from the city.

b) Your friend doesn't have that letter.

c) Those cherries are in the kitchen.

d) That is absurd!

e) These shoes are not comfortable.

f) That man is married – he is from Segovia.

g) This exam is not easy.

h) This is worrying, I don't have enough money in the bank.

i) This woman is very sad because her son doesn't have a girlfriend.

j) My friends live in these houses.

Check your answers in the Answers Section.

GUSTAR

GUSTAR	The verb *to please / to like*
PRONOUN	A word that replaces a noun.
OBJECT PRONOUNS	The words that mean *me, you, him, her, it, us, you, them* (me, te, le, nos, os, les).
SUBJECT	The person or thing doing the action of the verb in a sentence.
OBJECT	The person or thing on the receiving end of the action of the verb.
GERUND	The part of the verb that ends "ing".
PREPOSITIONAL PRONOUNS	a mi, a ti, a él, a ella, a nosotros, a vosotros, a ellos, a ellas

Now we come to an extremely important and useful verb.
You will study in this Module about the verb *to like*.

You can't go very far in a conversation in any language without this verb!
Talking about our likes and dislikes comes into all types of conversation and is fundamental to basic communication.

How long is it, after meeting someone for the first time, before you are asking them questions such as:

"Do you like football?" "Do you like travelling?"

You might be wondering why I am devoting an entire Module to one verb.

The reason is that gustar is a special verb, and works in a different way to any kind of verb that you have studied so far.

To understand how it works, we need to do things in stages.

Let me start by explaining what is meant by the **object pronouns** and how they are used. Then you will be able to tackle the verb gustar and understand how it works.

Right back in Module 1, you learnt about the subject pronouns. To save you looking back, I am going to list them again here for you in case you have forgotten them.

Yo
Tú
Él / Ella / Ello / Usted
Nosotros
Vosotros
Ellos / Ellas / Ustedes

This list differs from the one in Module 1 because of the inclusion of usted and ustedes, which you have subsequently learned about.

I hope you remember that these are the words in Spanish which mean *I*, *you*, *he*, *she*, *it*, *you* (polite), *we*, *you*, *they* (masculine), *they* (feminine) and *you* (polite plural).

I also hope that you remember how I explained that they are usually not used in Spanish.
This is because (unlike in English) we can know from the ending of the verb who is doing the action of the verb.
The ending is different for each person, so it is usually unnecessary in Spanish to use the subject pronouns.

In English we always use them, and we put them before the verb in order to show who is doing the action of the verb. For example:

I smoke (as opposed to anyone else smoking).
He goes out (as opposed to anyone else going out).

I hope all this makes sense – it should be somewhere there in your memory!

Why are they called subject pronouns?

Every sentence – in any language – has a **subject**.

The **subject** means the person (or thing) who is doing the action of the verb.

Consider:

Charlie gives the dog the food.

In this sentence, *Charlie* is the **subject** because he is doing the action of the verb – he is doing the *giving*.

Equally, the **subject** of a sentence could be a thing. For example:

The hammer slipped out of his hand.

In this sentence, *the hammer* is the **subject** because it is doing the *slipping*.

The **subject** of any sentence must (by definition) be a noun.
A noun is a person, a place or any object / thing.

Now, in any sentence, a noun can be replaced by a **pronoun**.

Consider the first sentence again.

We can say:

Charlie gives the dog the food.

But we can replace *Charlie* with the subject pronoun and say:

He gives the dog the food.

We would use *he* if it were clear who the *he* was referring to.

Imagine I meet you at the checkout in the supermarket and we started talking. You would be very surprised if my conversation with you went as follows:

"I am waiting for my wife. My wife has just popped back to the dairy section to pick up some eggs as my wife is going to bake a cake this afternoon. My wife will be here soon."

The only time I would actually say *my wife* would be the first time. On the other three occasions (underlined in the text) I would use the subject pronoun *she*, as it would be perfectly clear who I was talking about.

Equally, in the second sentence, I would never say:

The hammer slipped out of his hand because the hammer was heavy.

I would replace the "second" hammer with *it*.

So, subject pronouns are used in the place of nouns – nouns that are the **subject** of the sentence.

Understanding subject pronouns will help you now to understand **object pronouns**, which you need in order to be able to get your head around how *gustar* works.

What are **object pronouns**, then?

Let's go back to our first sentence:

> Charlie gives the dog the food.

Charlie is the **subject** of the sentence, because he is carrying out the action of the verb.

The **object** of the sentence is *the dog*, because (let's say the dog is male) *he / it* is on the receiving end of the action of the verb.

Actually, *the food* is also an **object**, but we are not going to worry about that now.

The **object pronoun**, then, as you have probably deduced, means the word we can use to replace the **object**, which in this case is *the dog*.

The **object pronoun**, then, would be *it*, *him* (or *her*, if the dog was female).

> Charlie gives *it / him / her* the food.

Here are the **object pronouns** in English and in Spanish:

ENGLISH	SPANISH
Me	Me
You	Te
Him / Her / It	Le*
Us	Nos
You	Os
Them	Les*

> * There are other **object pronouns** for the third person singular and the third person plural, but they are not used with *gustar* so you don't have to learn about them yet.

There is one further point to make about the **object pronouns**, and a very important one.

The position of the **object pronoun** in a sentence is different in Spanish than in English.

In other words, the word order is different.

In English we say:

Charlie gives *him* the food.

In Spanish, however, the **object pronoun** goes before the verb. Like this:

Charlie **le** da* la comida. (Literally, "Charlie to *him* gives the food.")

* Da comes from Dar, the verb *to give*.

The **object pronouns** always go before the verb.

This takes some getting used to. Although this is not the primary purpose of this Module, doing a short exercise here that gets you used to this idea of putting the **object pronouns** first will help you with what follows regarding gustar. So have a go at the brief Practice Activity that follows.

PRACTICE ACTIVITY SIXTEEN

If you find yourself getting in a muddle with the sentences that follow, then try the following simple method to avoid making a mistake. Translate the verb first, and then worry about who the **object pronoun** is referring to.

1. Based on what you have just learned about **object pronouns** and their position in a sentence, translate the following sentences from Spanish into English·

   a) **Os** compro un coche.
   b) ¿**Me** puedes ayudar?*
   c) No **te** entiendo.
   d) **Nos** llaman cada día.
   e) **Les** vendo (a ustedes) mi casa.
   f) **Les** pego cuando estoy enfadado.
   g) **Le** hablo en inglés.
   h) ¿**Te** puedo llevar a la estación?*

* **puedes** and **puedo** you should recognize from the last Module – they both come from the verb **Poder** which means *to be able*. This verb is very often translated using can in English.

Check your answers in the Answers Section.

Now listen to the fourth track on the second CD.

TRACK 4, CD2

Right, so what has all this got to do with the verb gustar?

Let me start by saying that gustar is a regular verb, in the sense that it follows the regular pattern of an AR verb.

So it conjugates like this:

Gusto	Gustamos
Gustas	Gustáis
Gusta	Gustan

However, gusto doesn't mean *I like*! And neither does gustas mean *you like*, etc.

Why not?

At the beginning of this Module, in the Key Grammar Terms, I gave you two translations of gustar – *to like* and *to please*.

The point about these two translations is that one is literal and the other is a meaningful (or sensible) translation.

Literally, gustar means *to please*.
In normal, colloquial English, however, we have to translate it as *to like*.

You will see what I mean in a moment.

For the moment, in order to understand how the verb works, I want you to think of gustar as meaning *to please*.

So:

gusto	I please
gustas	you please
gusta	he / she / it pleases
gustamos	we please
gustáis	you please
gustan	they please

A vital point – gustar is never used without an **object pronoun**.

In Spanish, then, when I want to say *I like* something, what I literally have to say is "Something pleases me" – the *me* being expressed by the **object pronoun**.

Like this:

> **Me gusta** el chocolate.

Literally, that means "chocolate pleases me", but translated meaningfully into English it means *I like chocolate*.

Notice how the third person singular is used – gusta. That is because it refers to chocolate, in other words, *it*.

When you want to say that somebody else likes something (i.e. not I), all you have to do is use the appropriate **object pronoun**.

Look at these examples:

Te gusta el café.	You like coffee (it pleases *you*).
Le gusta mucho el vino.	He / She likes wine a lot (it pleases *him / her*).
Nos gusta la película.	We like the film (it pleases *us*).
Les gusta la comida española.	They like Spanish food (it pleases *them*).

Get the idea?

The **object pronoun** (me, te, le, nos, os or les) tells us who likes something.

In the English translation then, the **object** actually becomes the **subject**. Consider our first example sentence again:

> **Me gusta** el chocolate.

In Spanish, *chocolate* is the **subject** and *I* am the **object** – "chocolate pleases me."

But when we translate it into English as meaning *I like chocolate*, it's the other way round – *I* am the **subject** and *chocolate* is the **object**.

If the thing that pleases you (i.e. the thing that you like) is singular, then we have to use gusta (the third person singular).

If, on the other hand, the thing that pleases you is plural, then we have to use gustan (the third person plural).

This is logical when you think of gustar meaning *to please*, because if what you like is plural you are going to say *they please me*. For example:

Me gustan los coches japoneses.
I like Japanese cars (they please *me*).

Le gustan las uvas.
He / She likes grapes (they please *him / her*).

Os gustan esos colores.
You like those colours (they please *you*).

So, whenever you talk about liking something in Spanish, you always use the appropriate **object pronoun** with either gusta (for singular things) or gustan (for plural things).

Like everything new, it takes time to get used to this.

The CD track and the Practice Activity at the end of the Module will give you the chance to put into practice what you have learnt here, and in the Progress Check that follows this Module there will be a lot of further opportunities to see and hear examples of the verb gustar.

First, however, there are a few final important points that need to be made about gustar and its use.

1.   When gustar is followed by a verb – in other words, when we say *to like doing* something – the infinitive of the other verb is used. For example:

Me gusta estudiar.   I like studying.
Nos gusta esquiar.   We like skiing.

In English, we use the part of the verb that ends in "ing" – it's called the **gerund**. (The word **gerund** actually popped up right at the beginning of Module 1 but hasn't been mentioned since. It will be dealt with in detail in the next Module.)

We say in English *to like doing* something, but in Spanish they say "to like to do".

So, if it's a verb that follows gustar, the verb takes the infinitive form. (I am sure by now you remember that the infinitive is the bit of the verb that means *to do*. Check the beginning of Module 1 if you need reminding.)

Notice how when gustar is followed by a verb - as in the two example sentences above - the part of gustar that is used is the third person singular.

That is because the verb (studying or skiing etc) constitutes an action, which is singular.
Literally "skiing pleases me" - the action of skiing can be described by the pronoun *it*.

Therefore, me gusta is used and not me gustan.

The easy way to remember when to use gusta and when to use gustan is to think that gustan is only used when whatever it is that you like is plural.

Any other time you are talking about liking something you use gusta

2. There is no complication with making question and negative sentences with gustar. Exactly the same rules apply that you have already studied in Module 7.

For a question sentence, the word order doesn't change.

¿Te gustan las patatas fritas?	Do you like chips?
¿Les gusta la casa?	Do they / you like the house?
¿Os gusta el profesor?	Do you like the teacher?

And for a negative sentence with gustar, you just have to put the no before the **object pronoun**.

No **le gusta** el ajo.
No **nos gusta** vivir en la ciudad.
No **me gustan** las obras de Shakespeare.

3. You may well have noticed that after gustar the article *the* is used.

In English we can say for example:

Do you like meat?

But in Spanish, it's necessary to say *the meat*.

> ¿Te gusta la carne?

Strictly speaking, it is incorrect to omit the article after gustar. However, there might be occasions when you hear Spanish people omit it when they speak.

Language evolves, and grammar mistakes can become accepted over time and incorporated into the language – often to the point where they are no longer classed as mistakes.

I strongly recommend, however, that you get into the fixed habit of putting the article after gustar.

Look at these further examples in which I have underlined the article each time:

No me gusta la cerveza.	I don't like beer.
Nos gusta el arroz.	We like rice.
Les gustan las montañas.	They like mountains.
Me gustan las patatas.	I like potatoes.

Each of the above sentences is translated without the article in English.

Bear in mind that sometimes in English we do use the article. It is possible to say:

> I like the potatoes.

But that doesn't actually mean the same as:

> I like potatoes.

The latter meaning is general, *I like potatoes* in general, but the former meaning is specific, *I like the potatoes* (i.e. these ones that I am eating here and now).

In Spanish, however, you always have to use the article, regardless of whether your meaning is general or specific.

4. Sometimes there is a potential confusion who le gusta(n) or les gusta(n) might refer to. This concept of potential confusion has come up before in the course. Consider this:

Le gusta(n) can actually refer to three different people.

It could mean *he likes*, *she likes* or *you* (usted) *like*.

And les gusta(n) can mean *they like* or *you* (ustedes) *like*.

If it's not clear from the situation who le gusta(n) or les gusta(n) refers to, all we do in Spanish is put the name or title (i.e. my father, Mrs. Bridges, the baker or whoever) of the person at the beginning.

However, anything put before le(s) gusta(n) that tells us who le(s) gusta(n) refers to must be preceded by the word "a" in Spanish.

Have a look at these examples below:

A mi padre **le gusta** la cerveza.	My father likes beer.
A María **le gustan** sus primos.	Maria likes her cousins.
A su profesor no **le gusta** enseñar.	His teacher doesn't like teaching.
A tus padres **les gusta** viajar.	Your parents like travelling.

This word "a" actually means *at* or *to*.

That "a" must always go before the name or title of someone that precedes the **object pronoun** used with the verb gustar.

There are also a set of what we call **prepositional pronouns** that can go before the other parts of the verb gustar, for emphasis.

They are:

A mi
A ti
A él / a ella
A usted
A nosotros
A vosotros
A ellos / a ellas
A ustedes

Now look at these examples:

A mi me gustan las manzanas
I like apples.

¿**A ti te gusta** fumar?
Do you like smoking?

A él le gustan libros de historia.
He likes historical books.

A ella le gusta jugar con sus sobrinos.
She likes playing with her nephews.

¿A usted le gusta España?
Do you like Spain?

A nosotros nos gusta comprar ropa.
We like buying clothes.

¿A vosotros os gustan las playas de Torrevieja?
Do you like the beaches in Torrevieja?

A ellos les gusta trabajar en la ciudad.
They like working in the city.

A ellas les gusta salir por la noche.
They like going out at night.

¿A ustedes les gusta comer en el jardín?
Do you like eating in the garden?

The meaning of these sentences doesn't change as a result of using the **prepositional pronouns**.

Using them simply has the result of emphasizing who it is that likes something.

5.   What happens when we want to say we like someone? This is where all the other parts of the verb gustar come in, and we have to think beyond just gusta and gustan.

Keep thinking of gustar as meaning *to please*. Keep applying the same logic as you have done up to now.

Consider this example:

   Me gustas.

Literally, then, I hope you can see that this means "you please me."
So, in English, that sense is *I like you*.

In reality, this meaning has a romantic ring to it.

This is quite confusing at first, and can take quite a while to get used to. It can be amusing too. If a Spanish person is rattling away in Spanish you can be left with the key question, "Hang on, who likes who?"!

So have a look at a few more examples and see if you can translate them without looking at the translation on the right-hand side.

Le gusto.	He / she likes me.
¿Os gusta?	Do you (plural) like him?
Te gustan.	You like them.
Me gustáis.	I like you (plural).
Nos gustas.	We like you.
Les gustamos.	They like us.

How did you get on?

I know it is confusing and difficult at first.
Probably the confusion and difficulty is not so much in understanding it, but in being able to use it correctly.

My advice is very clear on this one – don't worry about it too much.

It's certainly much more important at this stage to master the idea of how gustar works in relation to things, not people.
We all spend far more time speaking about <u>what</u> we like than <u>who</u> we like.

6.   There are some other verbs which function in a similar way to gustar. In other words, they use the **object pronouns** with the third person singular or third person plural of the verb.

For now, I am only going to mention one, the verb encantar. We can translate this as *to like very much* or *to love*.
When you saw the word, you may have thought of the English word *enchant*.

Look at these examples:

Me encantan los Beatles.
I love the Beatles. (literally, "they enchant me")

Le encanta escuchar música clásica.
He / she loves listening to classical music.

A nosotros nos encanta comer sardinas con ensalada.
We love eating sardines with salad.

A mis padres **les** encanta bailar en su habitación.
My parents love dancing in their room.

Now listen to the fifth track on the second CD.

TRACK 5, CD2

1.   Translate the following sentences from Spanish into English:

   a) No me gusta beber té por la mañana.
   b) ¿A ustedes les gusta su nueva casa?
   c) ¿Te gustan tus hermanos?
   d) A él no le gusta su profesor de español.
   e) Nos gusta trabajar mucho durante la semana y luego descansamos.
   f) ¿Os gusta el helado solo o con fruta?
   g) A mi hermano no le gusto.
   h) Me gusta comer mucho por la noche.
   i) ¿A tu mujer le gusta salir con otros amigos?
   j) A mis hijos no les gusta estudiar.

2.   Translate these sentences from English into Spanish:

   a) I like writing letters but I don't have time.
   b) They like the good life.
   c) We don't like English food.*
   d) He likes eating fish with a good white wine.
   e) Do you (plural) like travelling?
   f) Why don't you like cats?
   g) His father likes having dinner with his family.
   h) Their grandparents love going out in the car.*1
   i) You like lamb, but I like chicken.
   j) Miguel likes walking in the park with his dog.*2

   *   You have to say "the food English".

   *1 *in the car* here is translated by **con el coche**.

   *2 In this case, the verb *to walk* is **pasear**.

Check you answers in the Answers Section.

Welcome to the Third Progress Check. Having done two already, you will be getting used to how they work and my exhortations to use them to your own advantage. By now, I expect you will have found the best way to approach and do them, so I am not going to say a great deal here. Just keep in mind that they are here for your benefit, and that as they test everything you have studied so far, how well you do in them will directly reflect how well you are understanding and retaining what you are learning.

Having said that, I do urge you not to be too hard on yourself if you don't do as well as you hoped you would. Understanding the theory of what we have been studying is one thing. Remembering it and putting it all together when you are tested on it is something else.

Also, the exercises are naturally getting more difficult as they include more and more points that you have learnt. You are not only having to put into practice the things you have just learnt, but everything that you have studied throughout the course. So it's true to say that as your knowledge increases, so does your potential to make mistakes. You are bound to feel like kicking yourself over some things, but be patient. Rome wasn't built in a day, after all. That's a particularly good maxim to remember when it comes to learning a language.

One new thing here is the introduction of some more specific listening exercises. You will therefore need the CD for this Progress Check. My advice for these exercises is simple: just listen to the relevant tracks as many times as you need to in order to be able to answer the questions.

The reason for this is that listening is the one skill that no course can properly prepare you for. In order to be able to understand and follow the speed of a normal, natural Spanish conversation, your brain needs to go through a fairly long process of adapting to new sounds and relating them to meaning. There is no short cut for this. It is a hard reality, but the only way is for you to listen and listen and listen to as much Spanish as you possibly can. Even if someone knew every word in the Spanish dictionary, they wouldn't be able understand the first conversation they ever heard between two Spanish people. That mental capacity required to be able to follow spoken Spanish when you hear it only comes with a tremendous amount of time and practice.

PART ONE

Now listen to the sixth track on the second CD.

TRACK 6, CD2

1.   ¿Qué estudian?

2.   ¿Qué les gusta comer por la mañana?

3.   ¿Apariencia física?

4.   ¿Qué toman por la noche?*

5.   ¿Dónde duermen?

> * **tomar** means *to take* in the sense of taking something to eat or drink –
> here the question is referring to what they drink at night.

PART TWO

Translate the following sentences from Spanish into English:

1.   A mi hermana no le gustan las verduras.

2.   A esas chicas no les gusta estudiar.

3.   ¿Te acuestas temprano, no?

4.   ¿Puedes llamar a mi hermano?*

5.   Me aburro mucho en casa cuando estoy solo.*1

6.   Esa tienda cierra por la tarde.

7.   Lo siento mucho pero no puedo encontrar tu pasaporte.

8.   Estamos de vacaciones, pero no hace buen tiempo.

9.   ¿Te pierdes a menudo, no?*2

10. Mi padre no tiene un equipo preferido de fútbol, pero a mi me gusta el Real Betis.*3

11. Los profesores se sienten enfadados cuando los estudiantes no asisten a las clases.

12. Nos gusta comer con nuestros amigos cuando están aquí.

13. Es un buen profesor, pero es un poco estricto.

14. A tus hermanos no les gustan estas cerezas.

15. Vuestras hijas no son muy inteligentes, pero les gustan las clases.

* The verb **llamar** always takes the preposition "**a**" (meaning *to* or *at*) after it.

*1 **en casa** means *at home*.

*2 **a menudo** means *often*.

*3 **Real Betis** is the name of a Spanish football team.

PART THREE

Translate the following sentences from English into Spanish:

1. The lesson begins when the teacher arrives.

2. My name is Juan and I am from Costa Rica.

3. Do you (polite) have time this afternoon?

4. That is strange – those men don't have shoes.

5. Do you (polite plural) like meat or fish?

6. Those men drink brandy in the afternoon.

7. His parents can't come to the wedding.*

8. We go to bed very late because my husband works a lot.

9. He says he doesn't have a television.*1

10. These students are from the United States.

11. They like getting up early and eating on the beach.

12. Do you sit down when you eat?

13. I like this food very much – what is it?

14. Their friends go back to Italy every year.

15. It's cold today, isn't it? We can't play in that field.*

* The verb following *to be able* must be in the infinitive form.

*1 The verb **decir** must be followed by **que** (meaning *that*).

PART FOUR

Now listen to the seventh track on the second CD.

TRACK 7, CD2

THE PRESENT CONTINUOUS

PRESENT CONTINUOUS	The tense that expresses *to be doing*.
GERUND	The bit of the verb that means *doing*.
IR	The verb *to go*
VENIR	The verb *to come*
FREQUENCY ADVERBS	Words that express the frequency with which something happens.

There are two present tenses in Spanish, as there are in English.
This Module deals with the second present tense, and it's called the **Present Continuous**.

You have already learnt how to say *I do* something (e.g. *I eat, I sleep, I look at*, etc) in Module 1.
That is called the Present Simple.

The Present Continuous refers to the tense that expresses what *I am doing*. (e.g. *I am eating, he is sleeping*, etc)

It is called the **Present Continuous** because it refers to something that is a continuous action.

There are three uses of the **Present Continuous**, and we'll start by considering those uses.

1.   It expresses something that is happening at this particular moment in time.

For example:

    We <u>are eating</u>.
    They <u>are studying</u>.
    You <u>are watching</u> TV.

2.   It is used to express something that is on-going and continuing at the present time, but not happening at this exact moment.

For example:

    I <u>am reading</u> a very interesting book at the moment about Nelson Mandela. (but not right now)

    My dad can't play tennis at the moment as he <u>is having</u> treatment for his back. (but not right now)

    Have you heard about Matt and Nicole? They <u>are studying</u> Russian with their Russian neighbour! (but not right now)

3.   And sometimes, the **Present Continuous** is used to express something that is going to happen in the near future.

    I <u>am seeing</u> him tomorrow, so I'll pass on your message.
    We <u>are moving</u> in a couple of weeks, so things are pretty hectic around here.
    Her husband <u>is flying</u> to Italy tomorrow on business.

Those are the uses of the **Present Continuous** in English.
The first two uses are exactly the same in Spanish.

So once you know how to form the tense in Spanish (and it's not difficult) you will know when you have to use it, because you will use it on exactly the same occasions that you have to in English.

Forming the **Present Continuous** in Spanish is, as I have said, not difficult.

To do so, we need two things – the verb *to be* and the **gerund**.

Consider one of the example sentences above again:

    We are eating.

The *we are* comes from the verb *to be*, and the *eating* is the **gerund** of the verb *to eat*.

The **Present Continuous** is called a compound tense, because it is made up of two verbs – the appropriate form of the verb *to be* and the **gerund** of another verb.

Let's set aside the **gerund** just for a moment. You will learn how to form it in Spanish in just a moment. It is very easy.

Firstly, we have to think about the verb *to be*. I am sure you remember that there are two verbs for *to be* in Spanish. They are ser and estar.

To form the **Present Continuous**, which one are we going to use?

The **Present Continuous** always describes a temporary action or state of affairs.

I am eating or *they are sleeping* are temporary situations – nobody is going to be eating or sleeping for the rest of their life!
Look again at all the examples given in English so far in this Module, and notice how they all describe temporary actions.

That is the essential characteristic of the **Present Continuous** – the non-permanent state of affairs.

Therefore, for the **Present Continuous** we have to use the verb estar, which I hope you remember is used primarily to express location and temporary situations.

Let me remind you of the verb estar.

estoy
estás
está
estamos
estáis
están

So when you use the **Present Continuous**, you always use the verb estar.

Now for the **gerund**.

Right at the beginning of this course, in Module 1, the **gerund** was mentioned. Possibly you don't remember now. It is mentioned on the very first page.

The infinitive is the part of the verb that means *to do* something.

The **gerund** is the part of the verb that means *doing* something.

13

To form the **gerund**, it will help you to go right back to Module 1 and remember what you studied there about splitting the verb into two parts – the stem and the ending.

I hope that rings a bell!

Take mirar as an example. Look at what I have done to it here:

MIR-AR

To form the **gerund** of mirar, you need to make this split again, and remove the ending (i.e. ar).

Then add the ending "ANDO" onto the stem.

So, MIR-ANDO means *looking at*.

And if you put that together with the verb estar, you have formed the **Present Continuous**.

Estoy MIRANDO	I am looking at
Estás MIRANDO	You are looking at
Está MIRANDO	He / She is looking at
Estamos MIRANDO	We are looking at
Estáis MIRANDO	You are looking at
Están MIRANDO	They are looking at

The ending "ANDO" is the ending you need to put for AR verbs.

For ER and IR verbs, you need to add to the stem the ending "IENDO".

For example:

COM-ER	to eat
COM-IENDO	eating
VIV-IR	to live
VIV-IENDO	living

So there are actually only two endings that you need to learn for the **gerund**, because the ending for ER verbs and IR verbs is the same.

It's easy isn't it?

We are going to stop and practice in just a moment, but first there are three further points to be made about the **gerund**.

1. Some AR verbs have an "i" in the stem, so you have to be a little bit careful when you form the **gerund**. For example:

    Estudi-ar

Notice where the split is between the stem and the ending. The stem includes the "i", so the **gerund** is going to be:

    Estudi-ando

We are still keeping the rule and adding "ando" for an AR verb, but we are adding "ando" to a stem that includes the letter "i", hence estudiando.

Other AR verbs which also have an "i" include:

    Esquiar
    Anunciar
    Cambiar
    Limpiar
    Resfriarse

2. Some verbs have irregular **gerunds**. They are usually boot verbs which change from "o" to "ue" or "e" to "i" (see Module 10). Here's a list of five irregular ones:

    | poder | pudiendo |
    | morir | muriendo |
    | dormir | durmiendo |
    | pedir | pidiendo |
    | decir | diciendo |

Like all things that are irregular, they just have to be learnt.

3. The **gerund** part of the verb doesn't change. There is no singular or plural, or masculine or feminine to worry about or anything like that. The only thing you have to do is make sure you get the right part of estar and then follow it with the **gerund**.

It's as easy as that.

So, you have now learnt your second tense in Spanish!

Now listen to the eighth track on the second CD.

TRACK 8, CD2

PRACTICE ACTIVITY EIGHTEEN

1. Translate the following sentences into English:

    a) Estamos comprando un piso en Madrid.
    b) ¿Estás bebiendo mucho esta noche, no? ¿Por qué?
    c) Los primos de Juan no están escuchando la música.
    d) ¿Tiene usted mapa? Estoy buscando la plaza de Trafalgar.
    e) ¿Tu padre está trabajando en Londres, no?
    f) ¿Ustedes están buscando un perro?
    g) No podemos salir, porque el bebé está durmiendo.*
    h) Estoy preparando una paella con ensalada.*1
    i) ¿Estáis limpiando vuestra habitación, no?
    j) No estás estudiando mucho, según tu profesor.*2

    * **el bebé** means *the baby* – don't confuse it with the verb **beber**!

    *1 I hope you know what a **paella** is!

    *2 **según** means *according to*.

2. Translate the following sentences into Spanish:

    a) We are living in a big house.
    b) His brother is painting their living room.
    c) The dogs are barking in the garden.
    d) My children are studying French.
    e) You are singing my favourite song.*
    f) I am writing some letters to my friends.
    g) That cat is looking at the tree.
    h) My wife is visiting her father in hospital.*1

i)   Are you (plural) waiting for the bus?

j)   Our parents are not here. They are eating with some friends in a restaurant.

   *   Don't forget about the different word order in Spanish - you have to say "song favourite". (see Module 6)

   *1 In Spanish you have to say "the hospital".

Check your answers in the Answers Section.

Now, in the second part of this Module, we are going to look at another special verb. What you are about to study now is not difficult, and it will enable you to express a lot of things in Spanish.

We are going to look at the verb *to go*.

This is an important verb in any language, but especially in Spanish, as you will see.

The infinitive form of the verb is strange.

You learnt back in Module 1 that there are three groups of verbs in Spanish – AR verbs, ER verbs and IR verbs.

The verb *to go* is just the word ir.

In other words, there is no stem – just the letters "i" and "r".

As you may have imagined, it is an irregular verb.

Here it is in the Present Simple:

Voy
Vas
Va
Vamos
Vais
Van

This is easy to remember and easy to say. You will hear it on the CD shortly.

Now comes the important and curious thing about ir.

Its **Present Continuous** form (i.e. *I am going*, *you are going* etc) is the same as its Present Simple form.

13

In other words:

Voy	means	I go / I am going
Vas	means	You go / You are going
Va	means	He / She / It goes / He / She / It is going
Vamos	means	We go / We are going
Vais	means	You go / You are going
Van	means	They go / They are going

This verb is used so often in every day conversation.

It is especially used to express what we can call Future Intentions.

In English, as in Spanish, we use the expression *going to* to express something I intend to do in the near or distant future.

Have a look at the following examples in English.

They *are going to* buy a house in Spain.
I *am going to* write a book when I retire.
Are you *going to* call mum later? Give her my love.
We *are not going to* give up that easily!

Can you see how in each sentence an intended future action is expressed?

Stop for a moment and think how often you use this kind of sentence in English in your everyday life.

Learning how to express future intentions is going to greatly enrich your communication powers in Spanish.

Future intentions are expressed in Spanish in the following way:

Ir + "a" + infinitive

You have to take the appropriate part of the verb ir, then put the word "a"* and then the infinitive of the next verb.

* "a" is what is called a preposition. You will learn a bit about prepositions in Module 16. "A" means *to* or *at*. You may remember this from the previous Module.

Have a look at these example sentences, then, with ir expressing a future intention within this structure:

Voy a estudiar esta tarde.	I am going to study this afternoon.
Mi padre va a cambiar su coche.	My father is going to change his car.
Van a vender su casa.	They are going to sell their house.

Notice how the structure "Ir + a + infinitive" is used in each of these sentences.

Isn't it easy?

Before practicing what you have learnt in this Module, there are three further points to make.

1.   You might be wondering how you are going to know when, for example, voy means *I go* and when it means *I am going*, and when vas means *you go* and when it means *you are going* etc.

The answer to this problem is that there really isn't a problem!
You will know every time through your natural sense of the context.

In some of the sentences in the Practice Activity, you will find that the sentence could be translated as *go* or *going* – but if you had the whole context (and not just one sentence), it would be clear.
You really don't have to worry about that.

You will find that *going* and *going to* are much more common than *go*.

When the Present Simple translation is used (i.e. *I go*, *you go* etc), it is often used with **frequency adverbs** and / or time expressions. (You will learn about time expressions in Module 15.)

Frequency adverbs are the words which tell you how often someone does something, or with what frequency something happens.

Here are five of the most common ones – in frequency order – with translations:

always	siempre
often	a menudo
sometimes	a veces
rarely	rara vez
never	nunca

All these words express the frequency of events.

Look at some examples of how they are used with the verb ir:

A menudo **vamos** a la casa de mi tía.
Nunca **voy** a la playa.
Siempre **vas** a Londres cuando tienes dinero.

Can you see that the natural translations of these sentences into English means using *go* (the Present Simple) and not *going* (the **Present Continuous**)?

Here are the translations of the three sentences:

We often go to my aunt's house.
I never go to the beach.
You always go to London when you have money.

You will always be able to tell from the context how to translate or understand the use of the verb ir.

It will be clear to you at the time whether the sense is *go*, *going* or *going to*.

2.   The first person plural of ir (i.e. vamos) is also used to express the idea in English of *let's do* something.

When it is used in the future intention structure that you have just learnt (Ir + a + infinitive), it often means *let's + verb*. Consider:

Vamos a estudiar.	Let's study.
Vamos a limpiar la casa.	Let's clean the house.
Vamos a comer.	Let's eat.*

> * This sentence is spoken every day in a typical Spanish house. A mother bustles through into the living room where her children are playing and ushers them through with a clap of the hands and a "Vamos a comer!"

Again, your sense of the context will enable you to know the appropriate way to translate or understand what is being said – whether *let's do* something or *we are going to do* something.

Just vamos on its own simply means *let's go*.

You will often hear in Spanish the following words spoken:

"Venga, vámonos."

This means *Come on, let's go*.

Don't worry about the grammar behind this structure at the moment – it's complicated – but it is worth remembering the expression.

3.   Finally, there is one other verb in Spanish that is like ir in that its Present Simple form can be translated in two ways.

It is the verb venir, which means *to come*.
Here it is in the Present Simple, with its two translations:

Vengo	means	I come / I am coming
Vienes	means	You come / You are coming
Viene	means	He / She / It comes / He / She / It is coming
Venimos	means	We come / We are coming
Venís	means	You come / You are coming
Vienen	means	They come / They are coming

This verb probably reminds you of tener. It is extremely similar, but bear in mind that it is an IR verb, whereas tener is an ER verb. That makes a difference when it comes to how the first and second person plural forms are formed.

Now listen to the ninth track on the second CD.

TRACK 9, CD2

PRACTICE ACTIVITY NINETEEN

13

1.   Have a go at translating the following paragraph into English:

Mis padres van a comprar un piso en el centro de Madrid. Es un piso grande, y mi primo va a vivir con mi familia porque está estudiando biología en la universidad de Madrid y no tiene mucho dinero. Ahora está de vacaciones en Italia.

Ahora estoy viviendo con mis padres, pero pronto voy a vivir en un piso con unos amigos. Estoy trabajando en un restaurante en el centro de la ciudad, y el piso donde mis padres van a mudarse está un poco lejos. Va a ser más fácil* vivir con mis amigos en el centro.

Esta noche*¹ esos amigos vienen a mi casa. Vamos a cenar juntos, y mi madre va a preparar nuestra comida preferida. Mi padre no puede venir, porque va a la casa de sus padres. Mi abuela está bastante enferma.

Tengo dos hermanas. Se llaman Belén y Rosaria. Belén está trabajando en Inglaterra. Es enfermera, y le gusta mucho viajar. No está casada, pero tiene un novio inglés. Y Rosaria está escribiendo un libro sobre*² la historia de nuestra familia. Vive en Móstoles (cerca de Madrid) pero viene a la casa de mis padres esta noche también. Dice que*³ va a ser muy famosa en el futuro.

> * **más fácil** means "more easy", which we would translate as *easier*.
>
> *¹ **esta noche** – literally "this night", colloquially, *tonight*.
>
> *² **sobre** means *about*.
>
> *³ Remember that the verb **decir** must be followed by **que** (meaning *that*) in Spanish when the sentence goes on to say what is said.

2.   Translate the following sentences into Spanish:

a) They are coming to London this week.*
b) Are you going to Pablo's party tomorrow?
c) Let's go out tonight – I don't want to see the match.*¹
d) Your grandparents are going to sell their house, aren't they?
e) I am going to need a lot of money – can you help?
f) Is your (polite plural) daughter going to get married soon?*²
g) That car is going too fast.
h) My sister isn't coming, she doesn't like you.
i) I always go to my friend's house in the evening.*³
j) Are you (plural) going to clean the kitchen?

> * Don't forget to put "**a**", meaning *to*.
>
> *¹ Do you remember how to say *tonight*? Look at the previous exercise if not.
>
> *² *to get married* and *to be married* are not the same – check your dictionary carefully.
>
> *³ *in the evening* is the same in Spanish as *in the afternoon*.

Check your answers in the Answers Section.

ACCENTS AND VOCABULARY

ACCENT	The slanting line that sometimes appears above a vowel.
STRONG SYLLABLE	The syllable that is emphasized in the pronunciation of a word.
FALSE FRIENDS	Words which look similar to a word in the other language but which have a different meaning.

ACCENTS

An **accent** means the upward slanting line (left to right) that can appear above vowels in some words.

You will have noticed them throughout this course, and may well have known that they existed in Spanish anyway.

We will start this Module by explaining the use and purpose of **accents**.
For pronunciation purposes, it's necessary to understand when and why they are used.

For that reason, don't think that you can skip this Module on the basis that you are only interested in learning how to speak Spanish.

Accents are not only important for knowing how to write correctly.
They alter pronunciation, so you will need to know why they are used.

What an **accent** does is show us which **syllable** is **strong** in a word.

That may well not make any sense to you! Don't worry. The next track which you will hear shortly will clarify what is meant by the **strong syllable**.

It is difficult to explain in writing what the **strong syllable** means, because it's all to do with how a word sounds when it is pronounced.

This concept was touched on back in Module 11, when we considered the use of an **accent** to differentiate between estás (meaning *you are*) and estas (meaning *these*). Have a look back if you want to.

Every word – in Spanish or in English – has what we call a **strong syllable**.

Now listen to the tenth track on the second CD.

TRACK 10, CD2

Read again the pronunciation rules you have just heard on the CD and look at the further examples given here. Say the words to yourself out loud, keeping in mind what you have just learnt about the **strong syllable**.

1.   Any word that ends in a vowel ("a", "e", "i", "o" or "u"), or the letters "s" or "n" places the stress on the penultimate (second to last) syllable.

e.g.   libro
         hermana
         imposible
         supermercado
         comida
         dinero
         viven
         comemos
         padres

2.   Any word ending in a consonant (apart from "s" or "n") places the stress on the last syllable.

e.g.   profesor
         international
         arroz
         verdad
         director
         mirar (and all infinitives, because they all end in "r".)

3. Whenever either of these rules is broken, an **accent** is placed above the vowel that should be stressed.

Look carefully at the following examples, and see how either the first rule or the second rule has been broken in each case.

e.g.   canción (ends in "n", but the stress in on the last syllable, so the first rule is being broken, hence the **accent**.)

    lápiz
    médico
    cortés
    estáis
    estás
    opinión

When some nouns become plural they drop their **accents** because an extra syllable is added.
Take the last word in the list you have just read for example:

    opinión

Because it ends in a consonant, I hope you remember that to make it plural we have to add "es".
That was covered way back in Module 3.

So, it becomes:

    opiniones

The **strong syllable** is still the same one as when the word is singular (i.e. on the second "o"), but because we have added an extra syllable, it doesn't need the **accent** anymore.

It is now following the pronunciation rule, instead of breaking it, so the **accent** becomes unnecessary.

Sometimes this works the other way. The word examen (meaning *exam*) adds an **accent** in its plural form and becomes exámenes.

There are two further points to be made about **accents**:

1. **Accents** are used to differentiate between words that are spelt the same but have different meanings.

si	if
sí	yes
tu	your (see Module 4)
tú	you
el	the
él	he
solo	alone
sólo	only
mi	my
mí	me (in some cases, e.g. para mí meaning *for me*)
se	is the reflexive pronoun for the third person singular and plural (see Module 10)
sé	I know (it's the first person singular of the verb saber)

These are the most common examples of words in which an **accent** distinguishes between two separate meanings.

2.   Question words carry **accents** when used in question sentences.

¿Dónde está la estación?   (with **accent**)
Where is the station?

No sabe donde está la estación.   (without **accent**)
He doesn't know where the station is.

The second sentence is not a question sentence, so the word donde does not have an **accent**.

See how the same thing applies with these further example sentences:

¿Cuándo vienes a la fiesta?
(with **accent**)   When are you coming to the party?

No puedo decir cuando.
(without **accent**)   I can't say when.

¿Quién es ese hombre?
(with **accent**)   Who is that man?

No sé quien es.
(without **accent**)   I don't know who he is.

VOCABULARY

Learning vocabulary is a time consuming part of learning a language, but obviously you can't go very far without being able to remember words and expressions.

Words are the bricks of a language.

What follows in the second part of this Module are a few useful points about vocabulary in Spanish.

1.   You will have realized that a lot of words in Spanish are very similar to the English. This is because both languages have a root in Latin.

This means that you can recognize a lot of words when you see them written and know what they mean, which is extremely useful.

A very good example of this are all the words in English that end in "tion". The equivalent words in Spanish are always the same or virtually the same – they just substitute the "tion" for "ción".

Have a look at these examples:

    información
    estación*
    opinión
    reputación
    nación
    sensación

  * means *season* as well as *station*.

The list could go on and on.
Note that these words are all nouns, and you may remember from Module 3 that nouns ending in "ión" are always feminine.

Notice as well that they all have an **accent** in the same place, transferring the stress onto the last syllable.

2. You also learnt in Module 3 that nouns ending in "o" are generally masculine and nouns ending in "a" are generally feminine.

Now is a good time to list some of the important exceptions to this rule:

el sistema	system
el problema	problem
el programa	programme
el mapa	map
el pijama	pyjama
el día	day
el idioma	language
el tema	theme / subject
el drama	drama
la mano	hand
la radio	radio
la foto	photo
la moto	motorbike

It's a case of having to remember that these words are not the gender you would expect them to be!

3. Most shops that you would find in your average high street end "ería" in Spanish:

la carnicería	butcher's
la papelería	paper shop (not quite the same as a newsagent's, more like a stationer's that sells newspapers and tobacco as well.)
la ferretería	ironmonger's
la frutería	fruitshop
la pescadería	fish shop
la panadería	bakery
la pastelería	patisserie
la lavandería	launderette
la peluquería	hairdresser's
la librería	book shop

Notice that all these words are feminine, and they all carry **accents** on the last "i". You might be wondering why the **accent** is necessary – the reason is that "ía" constitutes only one syllable, not two.

4.   The last word in the previous list (librería) is actually an example of what
      we can call a **false friend**.

It has already been mentioned that many words in Spanish and English are
similar because the two languages share a Latin root. Usually, this helps a student
immensely, but **false friends** make life more difficult!

A **false friend** means a Spanish word which looks remarkably like a word in
English, but actually doesn't have the same meaning.

It deceives you because you think, "Oh, that must mean that!" and then you find
out that it doesn't.

Librería is an example of this.

It looks like it should mean *library*, but actually it means *bookshop*.

There are several **false friends** in Spanish, and it's worth mentioning some of
the more common ones here so that you don't mistake their meaning.

Some of them are highly amusing when you stop and think about the confusion
that they frequently cause for the language learner!

WORD	*LOOKS LIKE*	*REAL MEANING*
largo	large	long
fábrica	fabric	factory
sensible	sensible	sensitive
constipado	constipated	(with estar) to have a cold
pariente	parent	relative
éxito	exit	success
actual	actual	current
sano	sane	healthy
decepción	deception	disappointment
noticias	notices	news
diversión	diversion	entertainment
embarazada	embarrassed	pregnant
simpático	sympathetic	kind
suceso	success	event
espada	spade	sword

5.   In case you hadn't noticed, Spanish is quite a sexist language! The
      masculine plural form of some nouns is used for groups / people / couples
      that are mixed, i.e. that include both males and females.

For example:

Hijo means *son* and hija means *daughter*, but if I want to refer to both (i.e. *children*) I use the masculine plural word hijos.

Only if all my children were daughters would I use hijas.

Otherwise, I would have to use hijos, even if I had only one son and six daughters.

Here are some further examples of this:

padre	father
madre	mother
padres	parents
hermano	brother
hermana	sister
hermanos	siblings (brothers and sisters)
primo	cousin (male)
prima	cousin (female)
primos	cousins
abuelo	grandfather
abuela	grandmother
abuelos	grandparents

Now listen to the eleventh track on the second CD.

TRACK 11, CD2

PRACTICE ACTIVITY TWENTY

Now have a go at this Practice Activity in which you will practise some of the new words you have learnt in this Module together with grammar that you have learnt from the whole course.

1.   Translate the following sentences from Spanish into English:

a) ¿Vas a la frutería? ¿Puedes traer un par de limones?
b) A mis hijos les gusta estudiar francés con tu hija.

c) Tengo buenas noticias – mi mujer está embarazada.

d) ¿Estás loco? ¡No podemos robar la radio!

e) Estamos estudiando el mapa del centro de la ciudad.*

f) Vamos a visitar el hospital mañana.

g) La ferretería abre mañana por la mañana, pero cierra pronto.

h) ¿Qué programa vais a ver en la televisión esta noche?

i) Estoy constipado – voy a tomar unas pastillas.

j) Vuestra hermana está cantando una canción muy bonita.

     * **del** is the contraction of **de** and **el** (meaning *of the*) – there is a section on contractions in Module 16.

2.   Translate the following sentences from English into Spanish:

a) Where do your relatives live?

b) The boys in my class are not intelligent.

c) Do you have that photo of your girlfriend?

d) We don't want to use the bus – we need a car.

e) It's a long film – let's eat now.

f) There are a lot of students living in bad conditions.

g) That is an international problem.

h) Those children are going to buy bread from the baker's.

i) My father is angry because my mother is not going to buy beer.

j) That doctor has a good reputation.

Check your answers in the Answers Section.

WEATHER AND TIME

HACER   The verb *to do / to make*

In this penultimate Module, we are going to look at how to talk about the weather and how to tell the time.

These kinds of subjects are usually not particularly interesting, but are nevertheless extremely important.

They are also the kind of expressions that you can practise easily in Spanish. It is easy to make a comment about the weather to a stranger – apparently it's the most common topic of conversation when two people who don't know each other find themselves in a lift together!

And asking a shop keeper or a waiter what time their establishment opens or closes is something you can do just for practice – even if you don't need to know the answer!

That may sound crazy, but it's something I would readily suggest you do.

What you need more than anything else is the opportunity to practise what you learn. Until you actually put into practice the theory that you have studied in this course – by speaking to native Spanish speakers – you will never become confident.

You need to take every possible opportunity to practise your Spanish.

Let's deal with the weather first.

15

To talk about the weather in English, we use the verb *to be*.
We say, for example:

It is raining.
It is hot.
It is sunny.

This *it is* comes from the verb *to be*.

In Spanish, however, the verb *to be* is only used for a few weather expressions. More often than not, another verb is used, one which we haven't studied yet.

That is the verb hacer, which means *to do* and also *to make*.

So, there are two words in English expressed by the one in Spanish.

You will remember that the verb *to be* in English has two words in Spanish – ser and estar. Now, in the case of this verb hacer, we've got things the other way round – there are two words in English for the one word in Spanish.

Hacer means both *to do* something, and *to make* something.

So when in Spanish they say, *I do my homework* or *I make a cake*, they use the same word to express these two different things.

It is, therefore, an extremely important and common verb in Spanish.
And it's also irregular.

But before we look at this verb and consider how it is used in talking about the weather, let's look at some weather vocabulary and learn some expressions which are expressed the same way as in English (i.e. using the verb *to be*).

Firstly then, here are some weather words:

el tiempo	weather
el sol	sun
el calor	heat
el frío	cold
la lluvia	rain
la nieve	snow
el viento	wind
el cielo	sky*
la nube	cloud
llover (o to ue)	to rain
nevar (e to ie)	to snow

*This word also means *heaven*, as in *paradise*.

The two verbs at the end of the list are radically-changing verbs as indicated, but the funny thing about them is that they are only ever used in the third person singular – *it rains* or *it snows*.

You cannot say *I snow* or *they rain* etc, because of what the verb means. So:

llueve	it rains
nieva	it snows

Check back to Module 10 if you need reminding about radically-changing (or boot) verbs.

In Module 13, you learnt how to form the Present Continuous.

With respect to these two verbs, that would mean learning how to say *it is raining* and *it is snowing*. These expressions are formed exactly as you learnt in Module 13.

Está lloviendo.	It is raining.
Está nevando.	It is snowing.

The verb estar is used (as opposed to ser, the other verb meaning *to be*) because weather conditions are by nature temporary.

There is one other weather expression that is formed with the verb *to be* (estar).

Está nublado.	It is cloudy.

For most of the other weather expressions, we have to use the verb hacer.

Let's look at how hacer goes in the present tense:

Hago	means	I do / I make
Haces	means	You do / You make
Hace	means	He / She / It makes
Hacemos	means	We make
Hacéis	means	You make
Hacen	means	They make

You can probably see that it is only irregular in the first person singular.
But remember, any deviation from the pattern of normal verb formation – however slight – renders a verb irregular.

15

For this Module, you are only actually going to need the third person singular – hace.

In English, when we talk about the weather we use the verb *to be* and then put an adjective after it to describe what the weather is like. Consider:

> It is sunny.
> It is hot.
> It is windy.

Sunny, *hot* and *windy* are all adjectives.

But in Spanish, instead of using the verb *to be* + an adjective, they use the verb *to make* (hacer) + a noun.

> Hace sol.   (This is the translation of *it is sunny*.)
> Hace calor.   (This is the translation of *it is hot*.)
> Hace viento.   (This is the translation of *it is windy*.)

Instead of saying *it is sunny*, *it is hot* and *it is windy*, in Spanish they literally say "it makes sun", "it makes heat" and "it makes wind".

If you look back at the weather words listed earlier on in this Module, you will see that sol, calor and viento are all nouns.

This is another example of how languages have different ways of expressing concepts. It takes us back to something we considered earlier on in the course – the idea about literal and sensible translations.

It doesn't make any sense in English to say, "it makes sun" (which is what the sentence literally means.)
We have to express naturally in English the meaning that is being conveyed, which is *it is sunny*.

Here are the other key weather expressions in Spanish that use the verb hacer. I am sure you can work out what they mean based on the vocabulary you have been given above. At any rate, a full list of all the vocabulary and expressions follows to make it convenient for you to do the pronunciation exercises that come in the next track on the CD.

> Hace (mucho / un poco) frío.
> Hace (mucho) sol.
> Hace (mucho) viento.
> Hace (mucho) calor.

In all these expressions, the word that follows hace is a noun, not an adjective.

There are a few expressions relating to weather that use the word hay, which means *there is* and *there are*.

Hay niebla.	It is foggy.
Hay neblina.	It is misty.
Hay escarcha.	It is frosty.

To finish this section on weather, here is a complete list of all the words and expressions that you have studied here. You will need this for the pronunciation exercise that follows on the CD.

As there are no translations given, see if you can remember what the expressions mean. And if you come across any new expressions, see if you can work out what they mean by virtue of what you have learnt in this chapter.

¿Qué tiempo **hace**?
Hace buen tiempo / **Hace** tiempo bueno.
Hace mal tiempo / **Hace** tiempo malo.

Hace frío.
Hace sol.
Hace viento.
Hace calor.

el tiempo
el sol
el calor
el frío
la lluvia
la nieve
el viento
el cielo
la nube

llover
nevar
llueve
nieva
Está lloviendo.
Está nevando.
Hay escarcha.
Hay neblina.
Hay niebla.

Now listen to the twelfth track on the second CD.

TRACK 12, CD2

15

Now let's look at how to tell the time in Spanish.
It is not difficult.

In Spanish, there are three words for time – hora, tiempo and vez.
Each of them expresses something different.

In language, it's important to understand how one word can have more than one sense.
Consider the following three sentences in English, and notice how although they all use the word *time*, the meaning is different in each case.

1.   What time is it?
2.   Have you got any time tomorrow evening to give me a hand painting my house?
3.   How many times do you go to the gym each week?

For each of these sentences in Spanish, there is a different translation of the word *time*.

In the first sentence (and this is the one we need for the second half of this Module) *time* refers to the time of day (i.e. one o'clock, three thirty etc).
The Spanish word in this case is hora.

In the second sentence, *time* refers to a commodity, something someone can have.
The Spanish word in this case is tiempo (incidentally the same word as the word for *weather*.)

In the third sentence, *time* refers to an occasion when I do something.
The Spanish word in this case is vez.

I hope you can see what I mean about one word sometimes having different meanings.

This happens in all languages.

Although it might seem strange to you at first to learn that there are three words in Spanish that mean *time*, it is only because in English you are used to attaching to the word *time* all three of its different meanings.

For the Spanish mind (and this is quite logical when you think about it) it makes sense to use a totally different word for each situation.

This works both ways – there are single words in Spanish which have more than one meaning and more than one translation in English.

As you have learnt in this Module (and it appeared in the alphabet list as well in Module 2) the word tiempo means both *time* and *weather*.

For the English mind, there is no connection between time and weather, so why should the same word be used?

As a final example, think of the word *present* in English.
It can mean a gift, and it can also refer to now, as in the present time.
And the verb *to present* has yet another meaning, and is pronounced differently.

Why do we use the same word to express totally unrelated things?
I have no idea!

There are countless examples of this sort of thing that could be given.
The important point to understand (and you will have been doing so throughout this course) is that languages work differently from each other.

For the purposes of the second part of this Module, what you need to realize is that for the Spanish mind it is logical to have three different words for the three different senses of the word *time*.

The sense of *time* we are going to look at now is the first one listed above, that of the *time* of the day or night.

So we need the Spanish word hora.

¿Qué hora es?

This sentence, as you might have guessed, means *what time is it?*

The word es is used, which I hope you recognize. It comes from the verb ser, and means *he / she / it is*.

To tell the time in Spanish, the third person singular (es) and the third person plural (son) of the verb ser are used.

Es is used for any time for 1.00 to 1.59
Son is used for all other times – 2.00 to 12.59.

This is simply because the number one is singular, and all the other numbers are of course plural.

The other knowledge you need to learn to tell the time are the numbers and a few other words.

Quite possibly you already know some of the numbers in Spanish.

Just for now, here are the numbers from 1-20, and the number 25, as they are all you need to tell the time in Spanish. In the next Module, there is another section on numbers.

uno
dos
tres
cuatro
cinco
seis
siete
ocho
nueve
diez
once
doce
trece
catorce
quinze
dieciséis
diecisiete
dieciocho
diecinueve
veinte

The only other number you need is 25, for when you want to say 25 past or 25 to the hour:

Veinticinco

Let's start with how to say the exact hour, i.e. 1 o'clock, 2 o'clock, etc.

It's 1.00.	Es la una.
It's 2.00.	Son las dos.
It's 3.00.	Son las tres.
It's 4.00.	Son las cuatro.
It's 5.00.	Son las cinco.
It's 6.00.	Son las seis.
It's 7.00.	Son las siete.
It's 8.00.	Son las ocho.
It's 9.00.	Son las nueve.
It's 10.00.	Son las diez.
It's 11.00.	Son las once.
It's 12.00.	Son las doce.

This is all very straightforward. The only thing you need to take care with is 1 o'clock. Notice how it is singular and so es is used, as is la – es la una.

With all the others, son and las are used, as they are referring to times which are all more than one and therefore plural.

When it comes to expressing other times, there really is nothing difficult.

The Spanish words for *quarter* and *half* are cuarto and media respectively.

Literally, what is said in Spanish is "two and half" or "three and quarter" etc. Have a look:

Son las dos y media.	It's 2.30.
Son las tres y cuarto.	It's 3.15.

Consider some further examples and work out what the times are:

Son las siete y cuarto.
Son las nueve y cuarto.
Son las once y media.
Son las dos y cuarto.
Son las cuatro y media.
Son las diez y media.
Son las ocho y cuarto.
Es la una y media.

One thing to be careful about is confusing the number four, cuatro, with the word for quarter, cuarto.
They are easy to confuse – if you look carefully you will see that the difference between them is just the position of the "r" in the word (going before or after the "t").

The pronunciation of the numbers and all the words related to telling the time will be dealt with on the next track of the CD.

If you want to say another time "past" the hour (i.e. from 0-30 minutes on the clock), all you have to do is put the number of minutes past the hour (five, ten, twenty or twenty five) instead of cuarto or media. For example:

Son las doce y diez.	It's 12.10.
Son las tres y veinticinco.	It's 3.25.
Es la una y veinte.	It's 1.20.
Son las cinco y cinco.	It's 5.05.

15

Have a look at these further examples and try to work out what times they express:

Son las cuatro y diez.
Son las once y veinte.
Es la una y cinco.
Son las siete y veinte.
Son las ocho y veinticinco.
Son las diez y cinco.

Finally, then, we need to look at how to say times "to" the hour (i.e. from 30-60 minutes on the clock).

There is nothing difficult in this.

You just have to learn one more word – menos.
Menos literally means *less*, but in time expressions it's the equivalent of *to*.
Consider the following examples:

Es la una menos cuarto.   It's 12.45. (literally "one less quarter")
Son las dos menos diez.   It's 1.50.
Son las cinco menos veinticinco.   It's 4.35.
Son las seis menos cinco.   It's 5.55.

Notice how just as in English, when you express a time "to" the hour, you have to go to the next hour and take off the number of minutes that remain until that hour arrives.

Look at the following examples and, as before, work out what times they express:

Son las diez menos cuarto.
Son las doce menos veinticinco.
Son las ocho menos diez.
Son las dos menos cuarto.
Son las nueve menos veinticinco.
Es la una menos cinco.

What you have learnt here so far is how to say what time *it is*.
You also need to know how to say *at what time* something is happening.

To do this is very easy.

Instead of using the verb ser, all you have to do is use a la(s).

a la una	at 1.00
a las seis menos diez	at 5.50
a las nueve y veinte	at 9.20
a las once y cuarto	at 11.15
a las ocho y media	at 8.30

¿A qué hora…?	(At) what time…?
¿A qué hora vas a trabajar?	What time are you going to work?
¿A qué hora empieza la clase?	What time does the lesson begin?

Here are a couple of further useful expressions:

| sobre las nueve | at around nine (not specific or exact) |
| Son las diez en punto. | It's dead on ten / It's exactly ten (o'clock). |

That is virtually all there is to know about the time in Spanish, and I am sure you will agree it is not difficult.

Now listen to the thirteenth track on the second CD.

TRACK 13, CD2

PRACTICE ACTIVITY TWENTY ONE

1. Now have a go at translating the following sentences from English into Spanish to practise using what you have studied in this Module about time and weather. For all the sentences that include a time, don't just write the numbers! Write out the words in full in order to get used to using them.

a) We always get up at 6.00.*
b) Let's eat around 7.30.
c) It is cold in the mornings.
d) It's 8.25 and the programme begins at 9.10.
e) Now it is sunny but it is going to rain.
f) It is windy on the beach in the evenings.
g) The lesson is going to finish at 10.30 sharp.
h) Is it very hot in your town?

15

i) At 5.15 my friends have a Spanish lesson.[1]
j) You often go to bed at 11.00.*
k) It isn't very cold today.
l) At 4.35 his sister is coming here.
m) It isn't raining a lot – let's play in the garden.
n) It is 7.45 now, and I am going to my parents' house.
o) In the town where I live there isn't much sun in the winter.

      *   Put the frequency adverb first.

   [1]   a "lesson of Spanish".

Check your answers in the Answers Section.

MISCELLANEOUS

This last Module is a little bit different.

As the title of it indicates, it is not going to focus on one single subject.

Here you are going to learn some 'bits and pieces' that will help you to string together a lot of the things you have learnt throughout the course.

You will have been realizing throughout this course that Spanish as a language works quite differently from English in terms of how words are formed, how sentences are structured, and how concepts are expressed.

In this last Module you will see some more very practical and common examples of these differences.

Each different subject dealt with has a sub-heading.

PREPOSITIONS

Prepositions are a bit difficult to define. They refer to all the smallish words that often link parts of a sentence together.

Here's a list of some of the most common ones:

at	without
by	from
of	for
in	about
on	to
with	until

This is not an exhaustive list by any means, but the ones listed are certainly the most commonly used.
For the student of Spanish, however, there is a problem.

It is impossible to always translate prepositions in the same way.
Let me explain and demonstrate this.

If you look up the word *for* in the dictionary for example, you will find the words por and para given as translations of *for*.

However, you have already learnt (for example) that por la mañana means *in the morning*.

That does not mean that por means *in*.

It means that in certain expressions, the translation of a preposition might be other than what you find in the dictionary.

Let me try and make it absolutely clear.

The dictionary tells you that en means *in* or *on*, for example.
That is true.
But it is also true that there will be occasions when in English we say *in* and *on*, but in Spanish (if you translate the sentence) you have to use another preposition.

The example of por la mañana is a good one.

It is back to this business of literal and intelligent (sensible) translations.

A literal translation of por la mañana is "for the morning" because por means *for*. But that is a nonsensical translation, because we don't say it like that in English.

We say: *in the morning*.

If you have a big dictionary and look up (for example) the preposition *in*, it will tell you first the Spanish word is en.
Then there should follow a lot of examples.
In some of the latter examples, you will find that the word *in* is sometimes translated by another preposition in Spanish (not en).

Por la mañana is an example of what I call a fixed expression.

A fixed expression means a way of saying something that, when translated literally, doesn't sound natural.

It's a case of simply learning and remembering fixed expressions.

So, I hope you have learnt by now (because it has come up several times in this course) that por la mañana means *in the morning*.

That is a fixed expression – you just have to learn, accept and remember that when you want to say *in the morning*, that is how you have to say it.

Naturally, it is impossible here to give every single example of fixed expressions that include prepositions.

What can be done is to list some of the ones that you are likely to hear and use most frequently.

But before doing that, here is a list of some of the most common prepositions in Spanish with their 'usual' translations.

por	by / for
para	for
en	in / on
sobre	on / about
con	with
sin	without
hasta	until
a	to / at
de	of / from

Now look at the following points regarding fixed expressions with prepositions:

1. If you specify a time *in the morning*, *in the afternoon* or *in the evening*, then por la is replaced by de la.

For example:

Voy a mi casa a las ocho y media de la noche.
I go home at 8.30 at night.

Mis padres se levantan a las seis de la mañana.
My parents get up at 6 in the morning.

Por la mañana, por la tarde and por la noche are used then when the time is not specified and you are talking just generally about *in the morning*, *in the afternoon* and *in the evening*.

De la mañana, de la tarde and de la noche on the other hand, are used when you say specifically what time something happens.

2. Back in Module 2 you learnt the word cerca meaning *near*.

If you just say *something is near*, then all you need do is use the word cerca. But if you say *something / someone is near somewhere*, then you have to put the preposition de after cerca.

Look at these examples:

Nuestra casa está cerca.	Our house is near.
Nuestra casa está cerca de la pastelería.	Our house is near the patisserie.
Estamos muy cerca.	We are very near.
Estamos muy cerca de su oficina.	We are very near his office.

The same thing applies with the word lejos, meaning *far*.

El restaurante está muy lejos.	The restaurant is very far.
El restaurante está muy lejos de aquí.	The restaurant is very far from here.

3.   In English, when we talk about transport, we say someone travels *by plane*, *by train*, etc.

We use the preposition *by*.

In Spanish, however, they use the preposition en.

en coche	by car
en avión	by plane
en tren	by train
en autobús	by bus
en taxi	by taxi
en bicicleta	by bicycle

The only exception to this is:

a pie	on foot

4.   The words in Spanish for *before* and *after* are antes and después.

Like cerca and lejos, they take the preposition de after them if followed by a noun or a verb.

Look at these examples with nouns first:

Antes de la clase hago mis deberes.
Before the lesson I do my homework.

Vamos a comer juntos después de la película.
Let's eat together after the film.

In English we say *before / after doing* something.

In other words, we use the gerund. Have a look:

Before <u>eating</u> I like to drink water.
After <u>listening to</u> the news on the radio I go to bed.

In Spanish, the infinitive is used.
You can see that in the translation here of the two sentences you have just seen:

Antes de comer me gusta beber agua.
Después de escuchar las noticias en la radio me acuesto.

In fact, whenever the gerund (*doing* something) is used after a preposition in English, the infinitive (*to do* something) is used in Spanish.

The infinitive is used a lot more in Spanish than in English.
You will see this as you go deeper into the language.

5. The preposition para is used before the infinitive in Spanish when we want to express the idea in English of *in order to*.

Look at these two sentences in English:

I go to the baker's every morning to buy fresh bread.
I go to the baker's every morning in order to buy fresh bread.

We don't need to say *in order to* in this sentence, but it is quite acceptable if we do say it.

It means *with the purpose of*.
Why do I go to the bakers? I go *with the purpose of* buying fresh bread.

Whenever this idea is implied in Spanish, you have to put the preposition para before the infinitive.

This type of sentence is very common indeed.

Have a look at the following examples:

Voy a la academia para estudiar español.
I go to the school to study Spanish.

Estoy trabajando mucho para ahorrar dinero.
I am working a lot to save money.

Necesito un diccionario para buscar palabras.
I need a dictionary to look up words.

Vamos a hablar para resolver nuestro problema.
Let's talk to sort out our problem.

Quiero comprar unas patatas para hacer una tortilla.
I want to buy some potatoes to make a Spanish omelette.

Notice how para is used before the infinitive each time.

CONTRACTIONS

A contraction is simply the merging of two words into one for a phonetic reason.

When the preposition "a" is followed by the masculine singular definite article *the*, (in Spanish el) a contraction takes place.

"A" and el join and become al.

See how it works:

Voy al mercado con mi novia.
I go to the market with my girlfriend.

Vamos al restaurante para comer langosta.
We are going / Let's go to the restaurant to eat lobster.

It is not comfortable (phonetically) for the Spanish tongue to say "a el", because there are two similar sounding vowels together.
If they had to say "a el", it would break up the flow of the sentence.

So the sensible and easy thing to do is to form one word – al.

Exactly the same thing happens when de (*of* or *from*) and el find themselves together.

A contraction takes place to make del.

A well-known example of this is the Costa del Sol – "the coast of the sun".

Look at these further examples:

Es la casa del presidente.   It's the President's house.
Siempre compro pescado del mercado.   I always buy fish from the market.

When de is followed by a feminine noun, there is no need for a contraction.

Este vino es de la montaña.   This wine is from the mountain.

De la is perfectly acceptable in a phonetical sense.

Now listen to the fourteenth track on the second CD.

TRACK 14, CD2

Quite a lot has been covered in this Module already, so it's a good time to take a break, stop filling your mind with 'new' information and try and put into practice a little of what you have learnt here.

PRACTICE ACTIVITY TWENTY TWO

1.   Translate the following sentences into English:

   a) Hay un perro muy grande en la casa del profesor.
   b) Nuestros hijos van en coche al cine esta noche con sus amigos.
   c) Voy a ver las noticias antes de escribir la carta.
   d) Mis primos siempre van al colegio en bicicleta, pero yo voy andando.
   e) Tengo que ir a la casa de Miguel para recoger un libro que necesito para hacer mis deberes.*
   f) Su hermana está trabajando en una peluquería para ganar dinero y le gusta mucho.
   g) En la Costa del Sol hay muchos turistas que vienen de muchos paises.
   h) Sigo el ejemplo de mi hermano porque es muy inteligente y muy sabio.
   i) A mi abuelo le gusta bañarse a las diez de la noche.
   j) Para ir a Los Estados Unidos necesitas un visado.

   * **Tengo que** means *I have to* - this is covered in the second part of Module 16.

2.   Translate the following sentences into Spanish:

a) I always go to the office on foot because it is not far from my house.
b) Are you (plural) going to look for a house near the beach?
c) Near my house there is a beautiful park with flowers and trees.
d) Can you send the book to my brother's house? I go there often.*
e) It's a film about the history of Spain and it's very interesting.
f) Are you (polite plural) going to move after retiring?*1
g) We get up at 6 in the morning to study Spanish.
h) Do you (polite) like drinking coffee after dinner?*2
i) Before the lesson he is going to buy some pens.
j) They are going to say goodbye in the teacher's (masculine) house.

   *   **alli** is *there*.

   *1 *to move* and *to retire* are both reflexive verbs.

   *2 You have to say "after the dinner".

Check your answers in the Answers Section.

DAYS OF THE WEEK

Los días de la semana

lunes	Monday
martes	Tuesday
miércoles	Wednesday
jueves	Thursday
viernes	Friday
sábado	Saturday
domingo	Sunday
el fin de semana	weekend

The days of the week in Spanish do not need a capital letter.

In Spanish, when they say *on Monday* or *on Tuesday* etc, they don't use the preposition en (which you have learnt as meaning *on*).

You have to say:

el martes (literally "the Tuesday")

Look at these examples:

El sábado voy a la casa de mi hermana.
On Saturday I am going to my sister's house.

El miércoles tengo cita con el dentista.
On Wednesday I have an appointment with the dentist.

If you want to talk about something you do every Saturday, or Monday or whenever, in other words, a regular habit, you just have to make the sentence plural.

And you do that by making the article plural and saying los instead of el.

For example:

Los martes tengo clase de español.
On Tuesdays I have a Spanish lesson.

Los viernes por la mañana trabajo.
I work on Fridays mornings.

Sometimes you will see and hear the use of the word todos with the days of the week and related expressions.

Todos los viernes voy al pub.   Every Friday I go to the pub.
Todas las semanas voy al teatro.   I go to the theatre every week.

Todos is the masculine plural form of todo, meaning *everything* or *all*.
Todas is the feminine plural form.

MONTHS OF THE YEAR AND SEASONS

Los meses del año y las estaciones

enero
febrero
marzo
abril
junio
julio
agosto
setiembre
octubre
noviembre
diciembre

I don't think I need to write the English translations alongside!

Notice how the months of the year (like the days of the week) do not need a capital letter.

Here are the seasons:

la prima vera	spring
el verano	summer
el otoño	autumn
el invierno	winter

Look at these examples:

En verano en Málaga hace mucho calor.
It's very hot in Málaga in summer.

Siempre vamos a España en el invierno.
We always go to Spain in the winter.

Los jardines son muy bonitos en la prima vera.
The gardens are very beautiful in spring.

No me gusta el otoño, llueve mucho.
I don't like autumn, it rains a lot.

FREQUENCY ADVERBS

Do you remember anything about frequency adverbs?

They came up briefly in Module 13.

They are words which describe the frequency with which something happens.

Here again are the same common five that you learnt back in Module 13, but without translations. See if you can remember what they mean.

siempre
a menudo
a veces
rara vez / raramente
nunca

Their position in the sentence can vary, but generally frequency adverbs go in front of the verb (which often means at the beginning of the sentence).

Look at these examples:

Siempre tengo mucho trabajo.
A veces voy al teatro con unos amigos.
Raramente escucho la radio.

¿Con qué frecuencia…?

(literally "with what frequency…?") means *how often…?*

Look at how it is used:

¿Con qué frecuencia vas al cine?
¿Con qué frecuencia comes pescado?
¿Tu padre va a Barcelona con qué frecuencia?

THE PERSONAL "A"

Do you remember anything about the object of a sentence?
It came up in Module 12 when we talked about the verb gustar.
Have a look back if you need to refresh your memory.

When the object of the verb is a person, there is a special rule in Spanish.

Look at these examples and explanations in English:

I call Mark.   (Mark is the recipient of my calling.)
They are going to visit my mum. (My mum is the recipient of their visiting.)
Do you love your wife?   (Your wife is the recipient of your loving.)

In each of these sentences in Spanish, you have to put the preposition "a" after
the verb and before the object, i.e. the person.

Look at the translations of the three sentences above, in which I have underlined
the personal "a":

Llamo a Marcos.
Van a visitar a mi madre.
¿Ama a su esposa?

It is called the personal "a" because it is used when the object in the sentence is
a person.

Now listen to the fifteenth track on the second CD.

TRACK 15, CD2

MORE IRREGULAR VERBS

Here now is a list of some more of the most important irregular verbs in the present tense.

Some of them have already come up in the course, others will be new to you.

DECIR (*to say / tell*)

Digo
Dices
Dice
Decimos
Decís
Dicen

Do you remember this one? It is a boot verb.
It is followed by que when the sentence goes on to say what is being said. (e.g. *he said that…*)

DAR (*to give*)

Doy
Das
Da
Damos
Dais
Dan

Does this remind you of any other verb? It should do!

PONER (*to put*)

Pongo
Pones
Pone
Ponemos
Ponéis
Ponen

The first person singular looks rather like it might mean *I smell*, don't you think?

SABER (*to know*)

Sé
Sabes

Sabe
Sabemos
Sabéis
Saben

Saber means *to know* something, i.e. a fact / information.

Look at these examples:

¿Sabes a qué hora llega el tren?
Sabemos que no fuma en su habitación.
No sé su número de teléfono.

CONOCER (*to know*)

Conozco
Conoces
Conoce
Conocemos
Conocéis
Conocen

Conocer means *to know someone*, as opposed to knowing some information. Naturally it has to take the personal "a" after it.

Mi hermano conoce a un actor famoso.
Conocemos a tus parientes en Vigo.
¿Conoces a mi hermana? Se llama Nuria.

TRAER (*to bring*)

Traigo
Traes
Trae
Traemos
Traéis
Traen

VER (*to see*)

Veo
Ves
Ve
Vemos
Veis
Ven

In Spanish, ver la televisión is the translation of *to watch television*.

QUERER (*to want*)

Quiero
Quieres
Quiere
Queremos
Queréis
Quieren

Another boot verb, I hope you remember this one from Module 10.
Strangely, as well as meaning *to want*, this verb can also mean *to love*.
Te quiero (*I love you*) is the most common expression used between boyfriend and girlfriend, family members or close friends to express this particular sentiment.

NUMBERS

In the previous Module you were introduced to the numbers in Spanish.

Learning numbers 1-20 is actually the most time-consuming part, because once you've got them clear, there is very little else to learn.

After that, it is basically a question of learning the words for 30, 40, 50, 60, 70, 80, 90 in order to be able to get up to 99.

For numbers 1-20 you can refer back to the last Module and the section on time.

From there on, the numbers go like this:

veintiuno	21
veintidos	22
etc	
treinta	30
treinta y uno	31
treinta y dos	32
etc	
cuarenta	40
cuarenta y uno	41
cuarenta y dos	42
etc	

cincuenta	50
cincuenta y uno	51
cincuenta y dos	52
etc	
sesenta	60
sesenta y uno	61
sesenta y dos	62
etc	
setenta	70
setenta y uno	71
setenta y dos	72
etc	
ochenta	80
ochenta y uno	81
ochenta y dos	82
etc	
noventa	90
noventa y uno	91
noventa y dos	92
etc	
cien / ciento	100

How to spell the numbers isn't really very important, as when they are written they are usually written as numbers, e.g. "24" (not "twenty four").

CUÁNTO / CUÁNTA / CUÁNTOS / CUÁNTAS

In Module 7 you learnt some key question words.

One that you didn't learn at that time was cuánto, which means *how much* or *how many*.

If you have ever bought anything in a Spanish shop, then you are sure to know this one from the expression ¿cuánto es?, meaning *how much it is?*

The first thing you will notice is that there are four forms of the word.

The first two – cuánto and cuánta – are singular and (almost without exception) correspond to *how much* in English.

The second two – cuántos and cuántas – are plural and correspond (again almost without exception) to *how many* in English.

Look at these examples and see if you can work out what they mean:

¿Cuánto arroz quiere?
¿Cuánta fruta hay en la mesa?
No sabemos cuántos niños van a venir.
¿Cuántas patatas necesitamos para hacer una tortilla?

I hope you were able to work out that these sentences meant:

How much rice do you want?
How much fruit is there on the table?
We don't know how many children are going to come.
How many potatoes do we need to make a Spanish omelette?

TENER **EXPRESSIONS**

There are some English expressions with the verb *to be* (*I am*, *you are*, *he / she is* etc), that are translated into Spanish using the verb *to have* – tener.

We say in English:

to be hungry
to be thirsty
to be sleepy
to be hot
to be cold
to be lucky
to be successful
to be afraid

Each of these above expressions is translated using tener in Spanish.

Instead of saying *to be hungry*, in Spanish they say "to have hunger".
Instead of saying *to be lucky*, they say "to have luck", etc.

Look at the translations in Spanish:

tener hambre	to be hungry
tener sed	to be thirsty
tener sueño	to be sleepy (literally sueño means *dream*)
tener calor	to be hot

tener frío	to be cold
tener suerte	to be lucky
tener éxito	to be succesful
tener miedo	to be afraid

Be careful not to confuse the expressions tener calor and tener frío with what you learnt in the last Module about weather expressions.

Tengo calor means *I am hot*, and tengo frío means *I am cold*.
But hace calor means *it is hot*, and hace frío means *it is cold*.

The verb tener is also used in Spanish to talk about how old someone is.

In English, again we use the verb *to be* and say:

I am 30.
How old are you?

In Spanish they literally say, "I <u>have</u> x number of years."

Have a look at the examples:

Tengo treinta años.
Mi padre tiene sesenta y cuatro años.
Nuestra sobrina tiene nueve años.

And if you ask somebody how old they are, you have to say:

¿Cuántos años tienes? (literally, "how many years do you have?")

Tener que means *to have to*, as in some obligation that someone has to fulfill.

Have a look at these examples in English:

I <u>have to</u> go to the bank tomorrow.
You <u>have to</u> finish your homework before going out.
They <u>have to</u> get up early because they are going to Barcelona.

Notice how each of these sentences expresses an obligation – either self-imposed or imposed by someone else.

This idea of *to have to do* something is expressed in Spanish by tener que + infinitive.

Have a look here at the translations of the above sentences:

Tengo que ir al banco mañana.
Tienes que terminar tus deberes antes de salir.
Tienen que levantarse temprano porque van a Barcelona.

All these expressions with tener are all further examples of fixed expressions –
ways of saying something that, if translated literally, don't make much sense.

They just have to be learnt and remembered as they are!

REFLEXIVE VERBS

Reflexive verbs were covered in Module 10 along with boot verbs.
Do go back and have a look at that Module again to refresh your memory if you
want to – your brain has taken in an awful lot since then!

You have learnt how the reflexive pronouns (me, te, se, nos, os, se) are placed
before the part of the verb – for example:

Me llamo…   My name is…
Te levantas…   You get up…
etc

However, the pronoun can go on the end of the infinitive.
Consider:

¿A qué hora vas a levantarte mañana?
What time are you going to get up tomorrow?

No me gusta levantarme temprano.
I don't like getting up early.

In the first sentence, it would also be possible to put the pronoun te before the
vas, like this:

¿A qué hora te vas a levantar?

The latter way is more natural to Spanish people, and is therefore the option you
are more likely to hear.

Grammatically speaking though, both sentences are totally correct.

Now listen to the sixteenth track on the second CD.

TRACK 16, CD2

Now it's time to do the final Practice Activity of the course, which is based on what you have learnt in the second part of this last Module.

PRACTICE ACTIVITY TWENTY THREE

1.   Translate the following sentences into English:

a) El domingo mi amiga y yo vamos a la iglesia para cuidar a los niños.
b) Los jueves tenemos una reunión del comité en nuestra casa a las cuatro.
c) Tus hijas no tienen hambre pero tu hijo está comiendo una pizza entera.
d) Los chicos se van a despertar muy temprano mañana por la mañana para ir a bañarse en el mar.
e) ¿Sabes cuántas personas van a estar en la fiesta de Sergio?
f) ¿Con qué frecuencia llamas a tu novia?
g) Mi padre no quiere limpiar la casa porque es muy perezoso.
h) Queremos empezar las clases en enero – después de Navidad.
i) Van a saber los resultados del examen en la clase del lunes.
j) ¿Cuándo te vas a levantar mañana? ¿Desayunamos juntos?

2.   Translate the following sentences into Spanish:

a) At weekends I often go to Alicante by train to visit my girlfriend.*
b) There are eighty two pages that I have to read before tomorrow and I am sleepy. *1
c) Do you know the doctor's wife? She is quite tall and very attractive.
d) They are going to bring some bottles of Spanish wine tomorrow night.*2
e) How much milk do you want in your coffee? Let's eat some biscuits too.
f) My sister doesn't know when she is going on holiday.
g) It never snows here in autumn but it rains a lot, especially in November.
h) I don't know who is going to cook tomorrow because my mum is going to her friend's house.
i) I am not afraid if I am alone at home because I have a dog.*3
j) How often do you (polite) invite your friends to your house?

   *   *At weekends* is translated by **los fines de semana**.

   *1   *that* is translated by **que**, and don't forget the **de** after **antes**.

   *2   *tomorrow night* is **mañana por la noche**.

   *3   *at home* is translated by **en casa**.

Check your answers in the Answers Section.

PART ONE

Translate the following text into English:

Esta noche voy al cine con mi novia. Se llama Lydia, y tiene dieciseis años. Vamos a ver la nueva película de Tom Hanks, dicen que es muy buena. Quiero relajarme un poco porque el martes tengo un examen de italiano. No me gustan los idiomas, prefiero matemáticas y ciencias.

Lydia está en la clase de italiano también. Normalmente nos aburrimos mucho porque el profesor es mayor y tiene un estilo de enseñar muy formal. Habla casi todo el tiempo, y nosotros queremos dormir.

Me gustan los deportes y en mi colegio estoy en los equipos de baloncesto, tenis y fútbol. No soy muy alto, pero soy bastante rápido. Esta es la ventaja que tengo en estos tres deportes.

A Lydia no le gustan los deportes. Ella prefiere leer revistas, ir al cine, escuchar la radio y charlar con sus amigas. Es muy inteligente, así que* no tiene que estudiar mucho - tiene mucha suerte.

Vivo con mis padres en un piso cerca del parque. Durante el verano muchas familias van al parque los fines de semana para dar un paseo*1 y relajarse. El barrio donde vivimos es bastante agradable y hay muchos niños que a menudo juegan al fútbol en la calle. El pueblo donde vivo se llama Istoria, y aparte del parque también tiene unas playas muy bonitas.

Mi padre es periodista, y trabaja con el padre de Lydia, que es el editor del periódico. Se levanta temprano - a las seis menos cuarto - porque le gusta ver las noticias en la televisión antes de ir a la oficina. No me gusta levantarme temprano, pero todas las mañanas mi padre toca a la puerta de mi habitación a las siete.

* **así que** means *so*.

*1 **dar un paseo** means *to go for a walk*.

PART TWO

Translate the following sentences into Spanish:

1. What time do your parents get up in the morning?

2. Every Saturday their friends come to eat in our restaurant.

3. Those men don't like walking when it is very cold, they prefer to go by car.

4. We are receiving a lot of letters about the new geography teacher.

5. Do you (polite) have to go tomorrow? You can stay until the weekend if you want.

6. Who is going to buy the beer for the party?*

7. How often do you (polite plural) use the new computer in the office?

8. Does your brother know what time the train leaves?

9. I always go to the office by bicycle because I am too fat and need to lose weight.*1

10. In March my siblings are going to France to study French in a school in Paris.

11. I am going to bring the food to your (plural) house tomorrow afternoon.*2

12. Your sister's flat doesn't have a balcony, but it is quite big and very modern.

13. Don't your (plural) parents like living near the sea?

14. It's going to be difficult to put everything in the garage – let's see if we can leave some boxes in the bedroom.*3

15. This is absurd – he says he is not going to pay the money!*4

    *   Translate *for* using **para**.

    *1 *to lose weight is* **perder peso**.

    *2 You have to say in Spanish "tomorrow in the afternoon".

    *3 *to leave*, in this sense, is the verb **dejar**.

    *4 *he says that…*

PART THREE

Now listen to the seventeenth track on the second CD.

TRACK 17, CD2

	Gloria	Antonio	Carmen	Manuel
Age				
Number of sisters				
Where they live				
What food they like				
What time they get up				

PART FOUR

Now listen to the eighteenth and final track on the second CD.

TRACK 18, CD2

Course Postscript

A lot of theory has been covered in this course. How much you actually benefit from it will depend on how much time you spend working on transferring your new found head knowledge into practical working use.

Teaching and explaining the theory is as much as a teacher can do for a student. This course has presented you with a lot of information about how Spanish works – invaluable information. It has given you a platform – but what this course cannot do for you is make you speak Spanish. Applying what you have learnt is down to you. You can study this course over and over again in order to learn and remember all the theory covered in it – and reading and re-reading the Modules in sequence is something I fully recommend you do, but the point I am making is that that alone will never make you able to speak Spanish. Applying the theory – in other words, learning how to speak – is a different thing altogether. It takes practice, practice, practice and more practice, and although it can be very boring, there is no other way.

I cannot emphasize enough the importance of making yourself speak Spanish. If you are living in Spain, then you really have no excuses. You have to push yourself to try and speak as often as you possibly can. You have to be strong, prepared for setbacks. There will be confidence-sapping moments when you aren't understood or can't understand. All language students experience such valleys. Keep going. Don't let anything or anyone deter you.

I would like to share my personal experience with you.

This course has been borne out of my own experience of learning Spanish through living in the country. I went there alone, knew no English people, shared a flat from day one with two Spanish girls and worked with Spanish people in an office. There were times in the early days when I literally cried from pure frustration at not being able to communicate. I felt like a baby, although I had an adult mind. I knew what I wanted to say but couldn't say it! Not having any English people around me actually helped me, because it meant I had to learn quicker out of necessity. But in my learning curve there was a distinct turning point, and it's this I would like to share with you.

In the early days, I used to stay up every night until 1 or 2 in the morning with my dictionary and a couple of grammar books, but I hardly spoke to the people around me at all. I was a bit of a loner in fact – not because I wanted to be, but simply because I was so frustrated at being unable to speak, and I thought that it must be tedious for those around me who needed a great deal of patience to understand me!

After a few months I realized that the problem was as much about my character as anything else. I had to become brave and force myself to speak. For me, that meant stopping worrying about how I was going to sound, or about any mistakes I would make, or whether I would understand what was said back to me. I had to overcome all that – and simply speak. So I started going out and forcing myself to speak to those around me. I accepted invitations to go out, I invited people for meals, I spoke to shop assistants, café owners, neighbours, bus drivers – you name it. That was where I put the theory that I had learned about the Spanish language into practical use – on the streets.

I am not claiming that this is easy. But I would say to you that if you are serious about learning Spanish – and clearly you are to have got this far – that it is absolutely necessary to overcome whatever inhibitions you may have, and HAVE A GO!

Take every chance that comes your way to speak Spanish. Make opportunities for yourself. Ask things just for practice. Get used to trying. Be brave. Make the effort, and you WILL see the rewards. Nothing else will build your confidence.

Exhorting you in this way is as much as I can do for you! It's now down to you. I sincerely wish you all the best.

ANSWERS SECTION

HABLAR	BEBER	ESCRIBIR
hablo	bebo	escribo
hablas	bebes	escribes
habla	bebe	escribe
hablamos	bebemos	escribimos
habláis	bebéis	escribís
hablan	beben	escriben

TRABAJAR	VENDER	RECIBIR
trabajo	vendo	recibo
trabajas	vendes	recibes
trabaja	vende	recibe
trabajamos	vendemos	recibimos
trabajáis	vendéis	recibís
trabajan	venden	reciben

PRACTICE ACTIVITY TWO

1. eight

2. tomate (masculine) and carne (feminine)

3.

MASCULINE NOUNS	FEMININE NOUNS
alfabeto	familia
dinero	hora
gato	madre
libro	opinión
niño	
regalo	
tiempo	
zapato	

4.

   a) the potatoes

   b) an onion

   c) a tomato

   d) the vegetables

   e) the orange

   f) the bananas

   g) some fish

   h) some potatoes

   i) the grape

   j) the meals

5.

   a) el pescado

   b) una patata

   c) unas verduras

   d) las cebollas

   e) la carne

   f) unos plátanos

   g) los tomates

   h) unas uvas

   i) la comida

   j) una naranja

PRACTICE ACTIVITY THREE

1.

   a) Roberto's potatoes

   b) Maria's book

   c) Miguel's family

   d) Ana's shoes

   e) Ricardo's money

   f) Carlos's shop

   g) her students

2.

   a) la casa de Manuel

   b) los libros de Juan

   c) las cebollas de Alberto

   d) las naranjas de Elena

   e) el profesor de Alicia

   f) los amigos de Miguel

   g) el ordenador de Rosa

PRACTICE ACTIVITY FOUR

1.
   a) our lives
   b) his / her / their beer
   c) my clock
   d) my brother's car
   e) your sister
   f) your ideas
   g) his work / job
   h) his / her / their car
   i) your members
   j) his / her / their friends

2.
   a) su dinero
   b) nuestra tierra
   c) sus hermanas
   d) mi amigo
   e) tus regalos
   f) vuestros padres
   g) nuestras uvas
   h) sus esperanzas
   i) tu desayuno
   j) mis cerezas

PRACTICE ACTIVITY FIVE

1.
   a) We are teachers.
   b) The cat is under the table.
   c) We are near the beach.
   d) You are from Italy.
   e) Manuel is my friend.

f) I am in the kitchen with my girlfriend.

g) Our parents are in Spain.

2.
  a) Sus padres son profesores.
  b) Mi hermana está en el jardín.
  c) Estáis en la casa.
  d) Soy estudiante.
  e) Tus amigos son de Inglaterra.
  f) Tus amigos están en Inglaterra.
  g) Nuestra prima está casada.

PRACTICE ACTIVITY SIX

1.
  a) Mi padre tiene dos hermanas.
  b) Tengo (un) gato.
  c) Tus padres tienen (un) piso en Italia.
  d) Tenemos (unas) naranjas.
  e) Su madre tiene tres amigos / amigas.
  f) Tenéis (un) coche.
  g) Tienes una hija.

PRACTICE ACTIVITY SEVEN

1.   black, small

2.   old, oak, unshaven

3.   coarse, brown, tense

PRACTICE ACTIVITY EIGHT

1.
  a) We are Spanish and we live in Salamanca.
  b) My father is angry with my mother because the house is dirty.

c) There are many poor families who live in Brazil.

d) The history exams are not easy.

e) I have a new girlfriend.

f) We are in a very difficult situation.

g) In our house we have a famous Picasso painting.

h) There are two very thin girls in my class.

i) My brother has a very bad friend.

j) My sister's boyfriend is very good-looking.

2.

a) El jefe de mi padre es un hombre rico.

b) Es una película inglesa.

c) Tu profesor tiene un perro gordo.

d) Barcelona contra Real Madrid es un gran partido.

e) Su madre está muy feliz hoy.

f) La profesora no es muy buena.

g) Tenéis (una) casa pequeña.

h) Hay un pequeño problema con el coche.

i) El chico feo canta en la ducha.

j) La historia de tu amigo es muy triste.

PRACTICE ACTIVITY NINE

1.

a) Who speaks Spanish?

b) Where are the potatoes?

c) When do you work?

d) Why do you eat fish?

e) What ambitions do you have? / What are your ambitions?*

f) How is your mother?

*The second option here would be a more natural translation in English

2.

a) ¿Por qué trabajas en Londres?

b) ¿Tus padres cuándo estudian español?

c) ¿Cómo está tu amigo?

d) ¿Quién bebe cerveza?

e) ¿Dónde compra sus camisas?

f) ¿Qué comes por la mañana?

1.

   a) I don't have any brothers or sisters.

   b) Are you French?

   c) When do your children study?

   d) We don't live here, we are from Manchester.

   e) Don't you eat meat?

   f) Where is your brother?

   g) Are you in the office?

   h) No, I don't work in Brighton, I work in London.

   i) Who doesn't drink wine?

   j) Why don't you have a job?

2.

   a) ¿Tienes hora?

   b) ¿Dónde trabaja tu madre?

   c) No bebo café.

   d) No estudian italiano, estudian español.

   e) ¿Cuándo trabaja?

   f) No comemos carne, pero comemos pescado.

   g) ¿Hablas alemán?

   h) ¿Por qué escribe cartas tu padre?

   i) ¿Estáis en el jardín?

   j) ¿Quién habla español?

3.

   a) ¿Es guapa tu novia? / ¿Tu novia es guapa?

   b) ¿Dónde compras las patatas?

   c) No escribo libros, pero escribo unas cartas.

   d) ¿Es un coche nuevo? / ¿Es un nuevo coche?

   e) Su casa es muy grande.

   f) ¿Tus amigos beben vino tinto o vino blanco?

   g) ¿Cuándo estudian español?

   h) ¿No es buena profesora?

   i) Sus primos no tienen perro porque viven en un piso.

   j) El chico malo no vive con sus padres.

   k) Mi novia no es rica, pero es muy guapa y come chocolate.

l) ¿Quién lava el coche – tú o tu madre?

m) No como pollo porque soy vegetariano / vegetariana.

n) ¿Dónde está el mercado? ¿Está cerca?

o) ¿Tu padre es médico o periodista?

p) ¿Recibís regalos de vuestro tío?

q) Los amigos de mi padre no trabajan en una ciudad grande.

r) Su hermano es muy delgado porque no come mucho.

s) ¿Por qué no vendes tu casa? Es muy pequeña.

t) Nuestros hijos hablan francés – tienen un profesor gordo.

PRACTICE ACTIVITY ELEVEN

1.
   a) Are you Italian?
   b) Do you have two sisters or three?
   c) Do you write letters in the morning?
   d) Do you drink coffee or tea?
   e) Do you buy fish at the market?
   f) Do you live in a flat?
   g) Where are you now?
   h) Don't you smoke?
   i) Do you study a lot or a little?
   j) Do you speak Spanish well?

2.
   a) (Ustedes) no beben té.
   b) ¿(Usted) tiene mi diccionario?
   c) ¿Cuándo comen (ustedes) la cena?
   d) ¿Por qué tiene (usted) tres coches?
   e) ¿(Ustedes) tienen tres casas, no?
   f) ¿Cuándo habla (usted) francés?
   g) ¿Qué compran (ustedes) en el supermercado?
   h) Su amigo es muy delgado.
   i) ¿Sus amigos no trabajan en Inglaterra, no?
   j) ¿(Usted) estudia español ahora?

1.

a) SEGUIR

siguo   seguimos
sigues   seguís
sigue   siguen

b) CERRAR

cierro   cerramos
cierras   cerráis
cierra   cierran

c) MORIR

muero   morimos
mueres   morís
muere   mueren

d) VOLVER

vuelvo   volvemos
vuelves   volvéis
vuelve   vuelven

e) EMPEZAR

empiezo   empezamos
empiezas   empezáis
empieza   empiezan

2.

a) VENIR

vengo   venimos
vienes   venís
viene   vienen

b)   DECIR

digo	decimos
dices	decís
dice	dicen

3.

a)   ENCONTRAR

encuentro	encontramos
encuentras	encontráis
encuentra	encuentran

b)   DORMIR

duermo	dormimos
duermes	dormís
duerme	duermen

c)   QUERER

quiero	queremos
quieres	queréis
quiere	quieren

d)   SENTIR

siento	sentimos
sientes	sentís
siente	sienten

e)   ENTENDER

entiendo	entendemos
entiendes	entendéis
entiende	entienden

f)   PREFERIR

prefiero	preferimos
prefieres	preferís
prefiere	prefieren

PRACTICE ACTIVITY THIRTEEN

1.

a) LLAMARSE

me llamo   nos llamamos
te llamas   os llamáis
se llama   se llaman

b) LEVANTARSE

me levanto   nos levantamos
te levantas   os levantáis
se levanta   se levantan

c) PREOCUPARSE

me preocupo   nos preocupamos
te preocupas   os preocupáis
se preocupa   se preocupan

d) PREPARARSE

me preparo   nos preparamos
te preparas   os preparáis
se prepara   se preparan

e) LAVARSE

me lavo   nos lavamos
te lavas   os laváis
se lava   se lavan

f) ABURRIRSE

me aburro   nos aburrimos
te aburres   os aburrís
se aburre   se aburren

2.

a) SENTIRSE

me siento   nos sentimos
te sientes   os sentís
se siente   se sienten

b) SENTARSE

me siento   nos sentamos
te sientas   os sentáis
se sienta   se sientan

c) ACOSTARSE

me acuesto   nos acostamos
te acuestas   os acostáis
se acuesta   se acuestan

d) DESPEDIRSE

me despido   nos despedimos
te despides   os despedís
se despide   se despiden

e) DIVERTIRSE

me divierto   nos divertimos
te diviertes   os divertís
se divierte   se divierten

f) PERDERSE

me pierdo   nos perdemos
te pierdes   os perdéis
se pierde   se pierden

1.

   a) His / Her / Your / Their parents return home in the afternoon / evening.

   b) He / She is bored when he / she is alone.

   c) We get up very early.

   d) My son doesn't want to sleep when he drinks coke.

   e) Do you feel sad?

   f) I can't find the house keys.

   g) She washes (herself) in the morning.

   h) He / She has got two grandchildren – they are called Antonio and Maria.

   i) People die, it's a reality.

   j) Do you want to play in the park?

2.

   a) Su padre se llama Juan.

   b) No podemos estudiar hoy, no tengo mis libros.

   c) ¿Os divertís mucho en el parque, no?

   d) ¿Te acuestas tarde?

   e) Sus hijos no dicen mentiras.

   f) Me pierdo cuando no tengo mapa.

   g) No como mucho pescado, prefiero carne.

   h) ¿Os aburrís en la clase?

   i) Nuestro hijo es gordo, y nos preocupamos.

   j) Siguen las instrucciones del profesor.

1.

   a) You can sleep in this room.

   b) I buy these sweets every week at the market.

   c) That is the girl who eats a lot of chocolate.

   d) Those magazines are on the table in the kitchen.

   e) These oranges are very good – they are from Sevilla.

   f) I am sorry, but that is not logical.

   g) We want to buy this flat because it has a balcony.

   h) That parcel is a Christmas present.

   i) Those children always play football in the street.

   j) This is wonderful!

2.

    a) Esos chicos son de la ciudad.

    b) Tu amigo no tiene esa carta.

    c) Esas cerezas están en la cocina.

    d) Eso es absurdo!

    e) Estos zapatos no son cómodos.

    f) Ese hombre está casado – es de Segovia.

    g) Este examen no es fácil.

    h) Esto es preocupante, no tengo suficiente dinero en el banco.

    i) Esta mujer está muy triste porque su hijo no tiene novia.

    j) Mis amigos viven en estas casas.

PRACTICE ACTIVITY SIXTEEN

1.

    a) I buy you a car.

    b) Can you help me?

    c) I don't understand you.

    d) They call us every day.

    e) I sell you my house.

    f) I hit them when I am angry.

    g) I speak to him / her in English.

    h) Can I take you to the station?

PRACTICE ACTIVITY SEVENTEEN

1.

    a) I don't like drinking tea in the morning.

    b) Do you like your new house?

    c) Do you like your brothers and sisters?

    d) He doesn't like his Spanish teacher.

    e) We like to work a lot during the week and then we rest.

    f) Do you like ice-cream on its own or with fruit?

    g) My brother doesn't like me.

    h) I like to eat a lot at night.

    i) Does your wife like going out with other friends?

    j) My children don't like studying.

2.

    a) Me gusta escribir cartas pero no tengo tiempo.

    b) Les gusta la buena vida.

    c) No nos gusta la comida inglesa.

    d) Le gusta comer pescado con un buen vino blanco.

    e) ¿Os gusta viajar?

    f) ¿Por qué no te gustan los gatos?

    g) A su padre le gusta cenar con su familia.

    h) A sus abuelos les encanta salir con el coche.

    i) (A ti) te gusta el cordero, pero (a mi) me gusta el pollo.

    j) A Miguel le gusta pasear en el parque con su perro.

PRACTICE ACTIVITY EIGHTEEN

1.

    a) We are buying a flat in Madrid.

    b) You are drinking a lot tonight, aren't you? Why?

    c) Juan's cousins are not listening to the music.

    d) Do you have a map? I am looking for Trafalgar Square.

    e) Your father is working in London, isn't he?

    f) Are you looking for a dog?

    g) We can't go out because the baby is sleeping.

    h) I am preparing a paella with salad.

    i) You are cleaning your room, aren't you?

    j) You are not studying a lot, according to your teacher.

2.

    a) Estamos viviendo en una casa grande.

    b) Su hermano está pintando su salón.

    c) Los perros están ladrando en el jardín.

    d) Mis hijos están estudiando francés.

    e) Estás cantando mi canción preferida.

    f) Estoy escribiendo unas cartas a mis amigos.

    g) Ese gato está mirando el árbol.

    h) Mi esposa está visitando a su padre en el hospital.

    i) ¿Estáis esperando el autobús?

    j) Nuestros padres no están aquí. Están comiendo con unos amigos en un restaurante.

1.

My parents are going to buy a flat in the centre of Madrid. It's a big flat, and my cousin is going to live with my family because he is studying Biology at Madrid University and he doesn't have much money. Now he is on holiday in Italy.

Now I am living with my parents, but soon I am going to live in a flat with some friends. I am working in a restaurant in the centre of the city, and the flat where my parents are going to move to is a little far. It is going to be easier to live with my friends in the centre.

Tonight those friends are coming to my house. We are going to have dinner together, and my mother is going to prepare our favourite food. My father can't come, because he is going to his parents' house. My grandmother is quite ill.

I have got two sisters. Their names are Belén and Rosaria. Belén is working in England. She is a nurse and she likes travelling a lot. She is not married, but she has an English boyfriend. And Rosaria is writing a book about our family history. She lives in Móstoles (near Madrid) but she is coming to my parents house tonight as well. She says she is going to be very famous in the future.

2.
   a) Vienen a Londres esta semana.
   b) ¿Vas a la fiesta de Pablo mañana?
   c) Vamos a salir esta noche – no quiero ver el partido.
   d) ¿Tus abuelos van a vender su casa, no?
   e) Voy a necesitar mucho dinero – ¿puedes ayudar?
   f) ¿Su hija va a casarse pronto?
   g) Ese coche va demasiado rápido.
   h) Mi hermana no viene, no le gustas.
   i) Siempre voy a la casa de mi amigo por la tarde.
   j) ¿Vais a limpiar la cocina?

1.
   a) Are you going to the fruitshop? Could you bring a couple of lemons?
   b) My children like studying French with your daughter.
   c) I've got good news – my wife is pregnant.

d) Are you mad? We can't steal the radio.

e) We are studying the map of the city centre.

f) We are going to / Let's visit the hospital tomorrow.

g) The ironmonger's opens tomorrow morning, but it shuts soon.

h) What programme are you going to watch on television tonight?

i) I've got a cold - I am going to take some tablets.

j) Your sister is singing a very beautiful song.

2.

a) ¿Dónde viven tus parientes?

b) Los chicos en mi clase no son inteligentes.

c) ¿Tienes esa foto de tu novia?

d) No queremos utilizar el autobús - necesitamos un coche.

e) Es una película larga - vamos a comer ahora.

f) Hay muchos estudiantes viviendo en malas condiciones.

g) Eso es un problema internacional.

h) Esos niños van a comprar pan de la panadería.

i) Mi padre está enfadado porque mi madre no va a comprar cerveza.

j) Ese médico tiene (una) buena reputación.

PRACTICE ACTIVITY TWENTY ONE

1.

a) Siempre nos levantamos a las seis.

b) Vamos a comer sobre las siete y media.

c) Hace frío por las mañanas.

d) Son las ocho y veinticinco y el programa empieza a las nueve y diez.

e) Ahora hace sol pero va a llover.

f) Hace viento en la playa por las tardes.

g) La clase va a terminar a las diez y media en punto.

h) ¿Hace mucho calor en tu pueblo?

i) A las cinco y cuarto mis amigos tienen una clase de español.

j) A menudo te acuestas a las once.

k) No hace mucho frío hoy.

l) A las cinco menos veinticinco su hermana viene aquí.

m) No está lloviendo mucho - vamos a jugar en el jardín.

n) Son las ocho menos cuarto ahora, y voy a la casa de mis padres.

o) En el pueblo donde vivo no hay mucho sol en el invierno.

1.
   a) There is a very big dog in the teacher's house.
   b) Our children are going to the cinema tonight with their friends by car.
   c) I am going to watch the news before writing the letter.
   d) My cousins always go to school by bicycle, but I go on foot.
   e) I have to go to Miguel's house to pick up a book that I need to do my homework.
   f) His / Her / Your / Their sister is working at a hairdresser's in order to earn money and she likes it a lot.
   g) On the Costa del Sol there are many tourists who come from many countries.
   h) I follow my brother's example because he is very intelligent and very wise.
   i) My grandfather likes having a bath a 10 o'clock at night.
   j) To go to the United States you need a visa.

2.
   a) Siempre voy a la oficina a pie porque no está lejos de mi casa.
   b) ¿Vais a buscar una casa cerca de la playa?
   c) Cerca de mi casa hay un parque bonito con flores y árboles.
   d) ¿Puedes mandar el libro a la casa de mi hermano? A menudo voy allí.
   e) Es una película sobre la historia de España y es muy interesante.
   f) ¿(Ustedes) van a mudarse después de jubilarse?
   g) Nos levantamos a las seis de la mañana para estudiar español.
   h) ¿(A usted) le gusta beber café después de la cena?
   i) Antes de la clase va a comprar unos bolígrafos.
   j) Van a despedirse en la casa del profesor.

1.
   a) On Sunday my friend and I are going to church to look after the children.
   b) On Thursdays we have a committee meeting in our house at 4pm.
   c) Your daughters are not hungry but your son is eating a whole pizza.
   d) The boys are going to wake up very early tomorrow morning to go for a swim in the sea.
   e) Do you know how many people are going to be at Sergio's party?
   f) How often do you call your girlfriend?

g) My father doesn't want to clean the house because he is very lazy.

h) We want to start lessons in January – after Christmas.

i) They are going to know the exam results in the lesson on Monday.

j) When are you going to get up tomorrow? Shall we have breakfast together?

2.

a) Los fines de semana a menudo voy a Alicante en tren para visitar a mi novia.

b) Hay ochenta y dos páginas que tengo que leer antes de mañana y tengo sueño.

c) ¿Conoces a la mujer del médico? Es bastante alta y muy atractiva.

d) Van a traer unas botellas de vino español mañana por la noche.

e) ¿Cuánta leche quieres en tu café? Vamos a comer unas galletas también.

f) Mi hermana no sabe cuando va de vacaciones.

g) Nunca nieva aquí en otoño pero llueve mucho, sobre todo en noviembre.

h) No se quien va a cocinar mañana porque mi madre va a la casa de su amigo / amiga.

i) No tengo miedo si estoy solo en casa porque tengo (un) perro.

j) ¿Con qué frecuencia invita (usted) a sus amigos a su casa?

PART ONE

CANTAR	RESPONDER	SUBIR
canto	respondo	subo
cantas	respondes	subes
canta	responde	sube
cantamos	respondemos	subimos
cantáis	respondéis	subís
cantan	responden	suben

PART TWO

1. They sing on the bus.

2. You drink my wine.

3. María's grapes.

4. His / Her / Their brother climbs the mountain.

5. We look at the childrens' toys.

6. Our cat eats fish.

7. His / Her / Their mother cooks the vegetables.

8. We receive a present from our grandmother.

9. The teacher drinks tea with whisky in the lesson.

10. You eat some tomatoes.

PART THREE

1. Beben café.

2. Como mis naranjas.

3. El niño escribe una carta.

4. Nuestros amigos viven en Londres.

5. Trabajamos en España.

6. Mi hermana vende su casa.

7. Las madres compran pescado.

8. Tu amigo come unas uvas.

9. En la casa de Juan comen carne.

10. Miro a los gatos.

11. Bebemos unas cervezas en el jardín.

12. El profesor escribe en la pizarra.

13. El hombre en la casa come unos tomates.

14. Mi mujer / esposa prepara la cena.

15. Habláis italiano.

16. Tu padre come ajo.

17. El amigo / la amiga de mi hermana cocina arroz.

18. Como vuestras cerezas.

19. Sus primos reciben unas cartas de su tío.

20. La mujer de mi amigo bebe el vino y come unas cebollas y una patata.

PART FOUR

1. Nosotros hablamos español.
    We speak Spanish.

2. Yo trabajo en Valencia.
    I work in Valencia.

3. Vosotros vivís en el centro.
    You live in the centre.

4. Su primo escribe muchos artículos.
   His / Her / Their cousin writes many articles.

5. Tus padres comen carne.
   Your parents eat meat.

6. Mi padre cocina por la noche.
   My father cooks at night.

7. Nosotros respondemos a las preguntas de la profesora.
   We reply to the teacher's questions.

8. Tú bebes soda con tu whisky.
   You drink soda with your whisky.

9. Mis abuelos reciben flores de unos amigos en Francia.
   My grandparents receive flowers from some friends in France.

10. Él habla italiano.
    He speaks Italian.

11. Ellos cantan una canción.
    They sing a song.

12. Ellos reciben nuestros regalos.
    They receive our presents.

13. Mi hermana vende su coche.
    My sister sells her car.

14. Vosotros cantáis en la iglesia.
    You sing in church.

15. Tú vives con tu abuela.
    You live with your grandmother.

PART ONE

1. No hablo francés, pero mi novia es francesa.

2. ¿(Ustedes) beben té, café o zumo por la mañana?

3. Sus padres usan / utilizan mi ordenador.

4. Sus hijos no trabajan en la ciudad.

5. ¿(Usted) trabaja en una oficina?

6. ¿Coméis la comida francesa?

7. No tenemos dinero.

8. Beben leche por la mañana y vino por la noche.

9. ¿Sus estudiantes usan / utilizan ordenadores, o solamente libros?

10. Mi hermano escucha la radio cuando escribe cartas.

PART TWO

1. La niña gorda no come mucho.
   The fat girl doesn't eat much.

2. ¿Tiene (usted) hora?
   Do you have the time?

3. No trabajo mucho en la oficina.
   I don't work a lot in the office.

4. Tu novia está en la cocina.
   Your girlfriend is in the kitchen.

5. Carlos, ¿tu esposa es inglesa?
   Carlos, is your wife English?

6. Nuestros padres no viven en la ciudad.
   Our parents don't live in the city.

7. Comemos unas patatas.
We eat some potatoes.

8. Mi hermana es profesora.
My sister is a teacher.

9. Los primos de Roberto están enfadados.
Robert's cousins are angry.

10. No bebe café por la mañana.
He / She doesn't drink coffee in the morning.

PART THREE

1. We don't have a comfortable house, but the garden is very big.

2. The parents of my friend John don't buy fish at the supermarket.

3. The suitcases are small but they weigh quite a bit.

4. In my teacher's opinion, the maths exams are not difficult.

5. Our money is in a box under our bed.

6. I am sad because my brother is not married.

7. Most of the famous students at my school don't drink beer.

8. Our new lawyer is thin and a bit mad, but he doesn't live in the city.

9. I have a question – do we need onions?

10. Where is the rich boy with his Italian coffee?

PART FOUR

1. ¿Dónde estudias inglés?   (Informal)
   ¿Dónde estudia inglés?   (Polite)
   ¿Dónde estudiáis inglés?   (Informal, plural)
   ¿Dónde estudian inglés?   (Polite, plural)

2. ¿Cuándo trabajas?
   ¿Cuándo trabaja (usted)?
   ¿Cuándo trabajáis?
   ¿Cuándo trabajan (ustedes)?

3.   ¿Qué comes por la noche?
       ¿Qué come (usted) por la noche?
       ¿Qué coméis por la noche?
       ¿Qué comen (ustedes) por la noche?

4.   ¿Escuchas la radio por la mañana?
       ¿Escucha (usted) la radio por la mañana?
       ¿Escucháis la radio por la mañana?
       ¿Escuchan (ustedes) la radio por la mañana?

5.   ¿Vives en una casa o en un piso?
       ¿Vive (usted) en una casa o en un piso?
       ¿Vivís en una casa o en un piso?
       ¿Viven (ustedes) en una casa o en un piso?

6.   ¿Escribes cartas o correos electrónicos?
       ¿Escribe (usted) cartas o correos electrónicos?
       ¿Escribís cartas o correos electrónicos?
       ¿Escriben (ustedes) cartas o correos electrónicos?

7.   ¿Vendes tabaco?
       ¿Vende (usted) tabaco?
       ¿Vendéis tabaco?
       ¿Venden (ustedes) tabaco?

8.   ¿Respondes en español?
       ¿Responde (usted) en español?
       ¿Respondéis en español?
       ¿Responden (ustedes) en español?

9.   ¿Por qué tienes ordenador en tu garaje?
       ¿Por qué tiene ordenador en su garaje?
       ¿Por qué tenéis ordenador en vuestro garaje?
       ¿Por qué tienen ordenador en su garaje?

10.   ¿Tu profesor es italiano?
       ¿Su profesor es italiano?
       ¿Vuestro profesor es italiano?
       ¿Su profesor es italiano?

PART ONE

	Roberto	María
1.	medicina	filosofía
2.	sandwich de jamón	fruta
3.	alto y delgado	un poco gorda
4.	cerveza	té
5.	en el sofá en el salón	su propia habitación

PART TWO

1. My sister doesn't like vegetables.

2. Those girls don't like studying.

3. You go to bed early, don't you?

4. Can you call my brother?

5. I get really bored at home when I am alone.

6. That shop closes in the afternoon.

7. I am really sorry, but I can't find your passport.

8. We are on holiday, but the weather isn't good.

9. You often get lost, don't you?

10. My father doesn't have a favourite football team, but I like Real Betis.

11. (The) teachers feel angry when the students don't attend the lessons.

12. We like eating with our friends when they are here.

13. He is a good teacher but he is a bit strict.

14. Your siblings don't like these cherries.

15. Your daughters are not very intelligent, but they like the lessons.

PART THREE

1. La clase empieza cuando llega el profesor.

2. Me llamo Juan y soy de Costa Rica.

3. ¿(Usted) tiene tiempo esta tarde?

4. Eso es extraño – esos hombres no tienen zapatos.

5. ¿(A ustedes) les gusta la carne o el pescado?

6. Esos hombres beben brandy por la tarde.

7. Sus padres no pueden venir a la boda.

8. Nos acostamos muy tarde porque mi marido trabaja mucho.

9. Dice que no tiene televisión.

10. Estos estudiantes son de los Estados Unidos.

11. Les gusta levantarse temprano y comer en la playa.

12. ¿Te sientas cuándo comes?

13. Me gusta mucho esta comida – ¿qué es?

14. Sus amigos vuelven a Italia cada año.

15. ¿Hace frío hoy, no? No podemos jugar en ese prado.

PART FOUR

UNO Nuestros amigos no comen carne.
Our friends don't eat meat.

DOS ¿A ustedes les gustan los pisos modernos, o quieren ver una casa?
Do you like modern flats, or do you want to see a house?

TRES Esas manzanas están en tu bolsa con la botella de vino y unos plátanos.
Those apples are in your bag with the bottle of wine and some bananas.

CUATRO No me gusta estar sin dinero – quiero comprar muchas cosas.
I don't like being without money – I want to buy many things.

CINCO ¿Tienes tiempo libre esta tarde? Necesito tu ayuda con mis deberes.
Do you have time this afternoon? I need your help with my homework?

SEIS Tus padres no se levantan temprano porque no trabajan.
Your parents don't get up early because they don't work.

SIETE Hasta luego, y muchas gracias. Nos veremos mañana.
See you later, and thank you very much. See you tomorrow.

OCHO Mi novia está de vacaciones en Inglaterra.
My girlfriend is on holiday in England.

NUEVE Tengo dos sobrinos – se llaman Marcos y David – y una sobrina, se llama María.
I have two nephews – their names are Marcos and David – and one neice, her name is María.

DIEZ El trabajo de mi hermano es muy difícil y un poco peligroso.
My brother's job is very difficult and a little dangerous.

ONCE El profesor dice que tu hijo se aburre en la clase de historia.
The teacher says that your son gets bored in the history lesson.

DOCE No puedo encontrar tus gafas – ¿están en el coche?
I can't find your glasses – are they in the car?

PROGRESS CHECK FOUR

PART ONE

Tonight I am going to the cinema with my girlfriend. Her name is Lydia, and she is 16. We are going to see the new Tom Hanks film, they say it's very good. I want to relax a bit because on Tuesday I have an Italian exam. I don't like languages, I prefer maths and the sciences.

Lydia is in the Italian class as well. Normally we get really bored because the teacher is old and he has a very formal teaching style. He talks almost the whole time, and we want to sleep.

I like sports and at my school I am in the basketball, tennis and football teams. I am not very tall, but I am quite quick. That is the advantage I have in these three sports.

Lydia doesn't like sports. She prefers reading magazines, going to the cinema, listening to the radio and chatting with her friends. She is very intelligent, so she doesn't have to study a lot – she is very lucky.

I live with my parents in a flat near the park. During the summer many families go to the park at weekends to go for a walk and relax. The district where we live is quite pleasant and there are many children who often play football in the street. The town where I live is called Istoria, and apart from the park it also has some very beautiful beaches.

My father is a journalist and he works with Lydia's father, who is the editor of the newspaper. He gets up early – at a quarter to six – because he likes to watch the news on television before going to the office. I don't like getting up early, but every morning my father knocks on the door of my room at 7am.

PART TWO

1. ¿A qué hora se levantan tus padres por la mañana?

2. Todos los sábados sus amigos vienen a comer a nuestro restaurante.

3. A esos hombres no les gusta andar cuando hace frío, prefieren ir en coche.

4. Estamos recibiendo muchas cartas sobre el nuevo profesor de geografía.

5. ¿(Usted) tiene que ir mañana? Puede quedarse hasta el fin de semana si quiere.

6. ¿Quién va a comprar la cerveza para la fiesta?

7. ¿Con qué frecuencia utilizan (ustedes) el nuevo ordenador en la oficina?

8. ¿Tu hermano sabe a qué hora sale el tren?

9. Siempre voy a la oficina en bicicleta porque estoy demasiado gordo y necesito perder peso.

10. En marzo mis hermanos van a Francia para estudiar francés en un colegio en París.

11. Voy a traer la comida a vuestra casa mañana por la tarde.

12. El piso de tu hermana no tiene balcón, pero es bastante grande y muy moderno.

13. ¿A vuestros padres no les gusta vivir cerca del mar?

14. Va a ser difícil poner todo en el garaje – vamos a ver si podemos dejar unas cajas en la habitación.

15. Esto es absurdo – ¡dice que no va a pagar el dinero!

PART THREE

	Gloria	Antonio	Carmen	Manuel
Age	26	28	24	29
Number of sisters	three	none	one	two
Where they live	near Alicante	near Alicante	Madrid	Tenerife
What food they like	fish	paella	chicken	aubergine and salad
What time they get up	7.00	6.30	10.00	6.00

PART FOUR

No answer – the transcript for this track can be found in the CD transcripts section.

CD TRANSCRIPTS

TRACK 10, CD1

Mi nuevo coche.

El libro es famoso.

Están tristes.

Tu hermana es una persona feliz.

Cocinar es difícil.

¿Eres español?

¿Tu casa es grande?

Mi novio es delgado.

Nuestro profesor está enfadado.

Somos pobres.

Tengo un amigo inglés.

Tus padres son gordos.

Es un trabajo fácil.

¿Estás loco?

¿Estáis cómodos?

Vuestra madre es muy guapa.

Tu televisión es muy pequeña.

Tiene un buen trabajo.

Su familia es rica.

Los hijos de Carlos son malos.

TRACK 12, CD1

1. ¿Dónde vives?
   Vivo en Brighton.

2. ¿Tenéis hijos?
   No, no tenemos hijos.

3. ¿Tu madre bebe whisky?
   No, mi madre no bebe whiskey.

4. ¿Vuestro hermano habla español?
   Si, nuestro hermano habla español.

5. ¿Tu novia es delgada?
   No, mi novia es gorda.

6. ¿Cuándo bebéis cerveza?
   Nunca bebemos cerveza.

7. ¿Estás casada?
   Si, estoy casada.

8. ¿Dónde está la playa?
   Está cerca.

9. ¿Eres profesor?
   No, no soy profesor.

10. ¿Eres médico?
    No, no soy médico. Soy abogado.

11. ¿Estás enfadado?
    Si, estoy enfadado!

12. ¿Su padre trabaja en la ciudad?
    No, no trabaja en la ciudad.

TRACK 15, CD1

Hola, buenos días. Me llamo Begoñia. Soy española y vivo en Córdoba. Soy secretaria y trabajo en el centro de Córdoba.

Hola, soy Sergio de Madrid. Vivo con mi familia. No trabajo, porque soy estudiante de la universidad.

Me llamo Ana. Soy española, vivo y trabajo en Valencia. Tengo dos hermanos, pero viven en Salamanca con mis padres. Soy profesora de matemática.

TRACK 16, CD1

Hola, soy Carlos. ¿Cómo te llamas?

Buenas tardes. Me llamo Sylvia. Mucho gusto.

¿Dónde vives? Yo vivo en Madrid.

Soy de Alicante. Vivo allí con mi familia. ¿En qué trabajas?

Soy profesor de historia en un colegio. ¿Y tú? ¿Qué haces?

Soy estudiante de la universidad. Tengo clase ahora. Adios.

Adios, hasta luego.

Hola Carlos. ¿Qué tal?

Hola Sylvia. Estoy muy bien, gracias. ¿Y tú?

Bien. ¿Por qué estás aquí en el parque?

Hoy no trabajo, y hace buen tiempo, ¿no?

Si, hace calor. ¿Es tu perro?

Si, se llama Rocky. ¿Tienes perro?

No, tenemos dos gatos. Lo siento, Carlos, tengo clase. Hasta luego.

Hasta luego.

TRACK 2, CD2

¿Te lavas por la mañana?

Mis padres se levantan tarde.

¿Cuándo te acuestas?

¿Cómo se llama el pueblo donde viven ustedes?

Me aburro en la clase de matemáticas.

¿Cómo os sentís?

Nos sentamos en la cocina.

Su madre nunca se preocupa.

Nos perdemos en el parque.

Hola, me llamo Alfonso.

¿Tus hermanas se llaman Carmen y Lucia, ¿no?

No me siento bien.

TRACK 4 (2)

¿Te puedo ayudar?

Mi madre me compra caramelos.

La profesora nos habla en francés.

Su madre les regaña cuando está enfadada.

¿Le podemos llamar mañana?

Vuestros tíos os escriben en la Navidad.

TRACK 6, CD2

Roberto y María son hermanos. Viven en un piso en el centro de Málaga con sus padres, y ambos son estudiantes. María estudia filosofía y Roberto es estudiante de medicina. Quiere ser médico en el futuro.

Normalmente, comen juntos por la mañana. A Roberto le gusta comer un sandwich de jamón, pero María come solamente fruta.

Roberto es muy alto y delgado, pero su hermana es un poco gorda porque come chocolate por las tardes.

Su padre es profesor de matemática en un colegio local. Su madre es ama de casa y le gusta cocinar mucho.

Por las noches, a María le gusta tomar un te, pero Roberto prefiere una cerveza. Duerme en el sofá en el salón porque es un piso pequeño. María tiene una cama en su propia habitación.

TRACK 17, CD2

Hola, me llamo Gloria. Vivo cerca de Alicante con mi marido y nuestra hija. Soy secretaria. Tengo un trabajo duro y tengo que levantarme a las siete todas las mañanas. Tengo tres hermanas y un hermano – todos viven en Málaga porque mi familia es de Málaga. En Málaga tenemos comida muy buena, y me gusta mucho todos los tipos de pescado que hay.

Mi marido se llama Antonio y tiene veintiocho años – dos más que yo. Nos amamos mucho. Su familia no es grande, tiene solamente un hermano que se llama Ricardo. A mi marido le gusta mucho la paella, que es la comida más famosa en España. Es cocinero, así que en casa comemos muy bien. Tengo suerte que mi marido es cocinero, no tengo que preparar la comida todas las noches. Trabaja mucho, y se levanta a las seis y media.

Tengo una buena amiga que vive y trabaja en Madrid. Se llama Carmen, y tiene un novio que es periodista en Tenerife. Es muy guapo y se llama Manuel, pero no pueden verse mucho. Carmen tiene veinticuatro años y Manuel veintinueve. No se si van a casarse en el futuro.

Es curioso, Manuel tiene dos hermanas que viven en España, y una conoce a la hermana de Carmen porque trabajan para la misma compañia.

A veces Carmen y Manuel vienen a Alicante para comer la comida de mi marido. A ella le gusta mucho el pollo, pero él es vegetariano y prefiere berenjena y ensalada. El trabajo de Carmen no es difícil – empieza a la una y se levanta a las diez. Pero el pobre Manuel tiene mucho estrés con el periódico y tiene que levantarse a las seis.

TRACK 18, CD2

Estoy viviendo en un barrio de Málaga que se llama Molinillo. Está cerca del estadio de fútbol, La Rosaleda, y también está al lado del río. Hay un mercado cerca del piso donde vivo, y puedo comprar todo lo que necesito allí. También, los domingos hay un mercado abierto donde puedes comprar muchas cosas.

Me gusta Málaga, porque tiene un ambiente especial y hay mar. Vivo con mi mujer y mi hija. Se llama Luna y tiene cinco años. Es morena y muy guapa, como su madre. Les quiero a mi familia muchísimo, y los fines de semana cuando no estoy trabajando siempre salimos juntos para dar un paseo en el parque o para tomar un helado. A mi hija le gusta mucho el helado.

Trabajo para una compañia de seguro. La verdad es que no me gusta mucho, porque tengo que trabajar hasta las siete de la tarde todos los días. Pienso que es demasiado. La oficina donde trabajo está en el centro de la ciudad, pero voy a pie siempre porque el centro de Málaga no es grande y es muy difícil aparcar. Salgo de mi casa a las ocho y media, y tardo veinte minutos en llegar.

En verano, hace mucho calor en Málaga. La verdad es que a mi me gusta mucho el calor, pero en agosto es demasiado. Sudas mucho, no hay viento y te sientes muy incómodo. También hay muchas cucarachas en la calle, ¡cosa que a mi mujer no le gusta en absoluto!

En el verano me gusta beber cerveza o tinto de verano. Tinto de verano es una bebida típica de España, es vino tinto con gaseosa, hielo y un trozo de limón. Es muy refrescante. En el invierno, prefiero beber vino tinto, porque hace frío por las noches. De hecho, no hace mucho frío, pero mi casa no tiene calefacción, así que a veces tenemos frío.

Tengo dos hermanas, pero ambas están casadas con madrileños y entonces viven en Madrid. En total, mis padres tienen cuatro nietos y son muy felices. Mis hermanas dicen que echan de menos a Málaga siempre.

En Madrid no hay playa, y en el invierno hace mucho frío. Vienen dos o tres veces al año, y también a menudo voy a Madrid para mi trabajo, así que nos vemos bastante.

Me gustan mucho los deportes. Mi equipo preferido de fútbol es Málaga, por supuesto, pero me gusta también Real Madrid, porque conozco a uno de los jugadores. Me interesa también la política y la situación international. A menudo leo periódicos y revistas para saber lo que está pasando en el mundo.